The War in Plymouth: Destruction and a New Beginning

A Community Project from The Word Machine CIC

Supported by

The National Lottery®
through the Heritage Lottery Fund

heritage
lottery fund

First published 2015

Copyright © The Word Machine CIC, 2015

The right of The Word Machine CIC to be
identified as the author of this work has been asserted by
it in accordance with the Copyright,
Designs and Patents Act 1988.

A catalogue record for this book is available
from the British Library.

ISBN: 9780957629455

Cover design by www.deluxe7.com

Printed and bound in the UK,
by Latimer Trend & Co. Ltd., Plymouth, Devon.

Foreword

The War In Plymouth: Destruction and a New Beginning
was a community project conducted by The Word Machine
Community Interest Company over a two-year period from
2013 to 2015, supported by the Heritage Lottery Fund.
The purpose of the project was to conduct an oral history
of the Blitz in Plymouth during World War Two, and the
subsequent rebuilding of the city in the ten years from 1945
to 1955. This book represents a sample of the fascinating
findings we have made during the project. The full oral
history recordings are now in the safe hands of the Plymouth
and West Devon Record Office. To access the complete
written transcripts and find information on how to listen
to the interviews themselves, please go to our website at:
www.thewordmachine.org.

Inevitably, given the period under investigation, our
interviewees ranged in ages from 71 to 97. I would like first
and foremost to thank all of them for their time, patience
and fortitude in reliving such an extraordinary but harrowing
period in the life of Plymouth and its residents.

I would also like to thank the many supporters,
volunteers and associates who have helped to make this
project such a fascinating success. In particular, I would like
to thank Tony Davey of Plymouth City Museum and Art
Gallery; Professor Kevin Jefferys and Kayleigh Luscombe
of Plymouth University; Matthew Pontin and Jon Blyth of
Fotonow CIC, together with their photographers Balázs
Turós and Jake McPherson; our patient and ever helpful
project manager at the Heritage Lottery Fund, Helen
Wheatley; Plymouth historian Chris Robinson; our many
volunteer interviewees and transcribers (who are listed at
the back of this book); and Tamsin Griffiths from
The Word Machine, who has led the project and
overseen the production of the book.

Simon Petherick

Director, The Word Machine CIC, October 2015

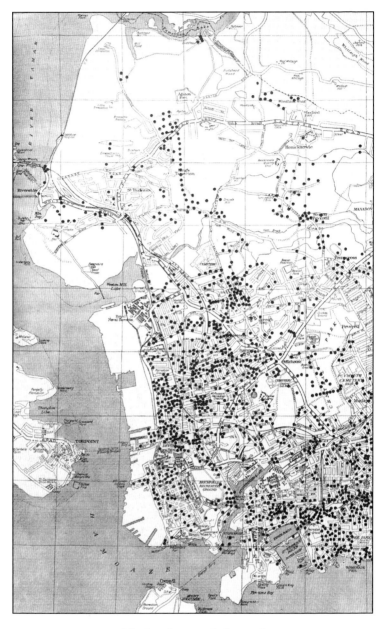

The bomb map of Plymouth

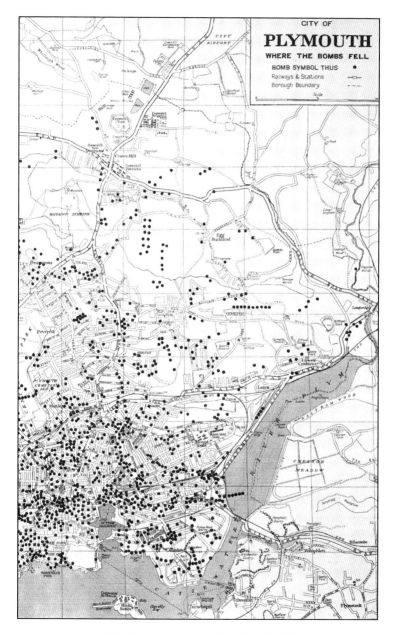

Black dots represent where bombs fell

The War in Plymouth

Evaluation Report Outline by Dr Kayleigh Luscombe, Oral Historian to the project

The Oral History Recordings

The project collated 60 oral history recordings that are forming part of a new archive deposited at the Plymouth and West Devon Record Office.

There is a successful gender balance within the interview collection with 30 interviews recorded with male participants and 30 recorded with female participants. Due to the theme of the project, participants were all over 71 years of age. People aged in their 80s formed the largest group, accounting for half of the interviews (30 of the 60 recordings). This was followed by people in their 70s, which accounted for 20 interviews. Participants in their 90s accounted for 10 interviews.

Overall, the project has achieved a fair balance of interviews in locations across Plymouth and surrounding areas. PL3 contained the greatest number of participants (12), which is not surprising as it is one of the largest postal code areas in the city. This was followed by PL1 (10) and then PL6 and PL7 (7 from each).

The breakdown of interview location is as follows:

Postcode	Districts covered	Total interviews
PL1	Devonport, The Hoe, Millbridge, Stoke, Stonehouse	10
PL2	Beacon Park, Ford, Keyham, Stoke, North Prospect, Pennycross, Home Park	4
PL3	Efford, Hartley, Laira, Mannamead, Milehouse, Peverell, Higher Compton	12
PL4	Barbican, Lipson, Mount Gould, Mannamead, Mutley, Prince Rock	6
PL5	Crownhill, Ernesettle, Honicknowle, Whitleigh, St. Budeaux, Tamerton Foliot	2
PL6	Derriford, Thornbury, Eggbuckland, Estover, Roborough, Southway	7
PL7	Plympton, Chaddlewood, Sparkwell	7
PL8	Brixton, Newton Ferrers, Noss Mayo, Yealmpton	1
PL9	Plymstock, Oreston, Heybrook Bay, Mount Batten, Wembury	5
PL10	Cawsand, Cremyll, Freathy, Kingsand, Millbrook	1
PL11	Torpoint, Antony, Crafthole, Downderry, Seaton, Sheviock, St John	1
PL12	Saltash, Portwrinkle, Landrake, St Germans, Tideford	1
PL17	Callington, Ashton, Bray Shop, Kelly Bray, South Hill	1
TA3	Henlade, Taunton, Somerset	1
PL21	Ivybridge, Ermington	1

Interview themes

Within the 'early years' theme, over 78% of interviewees had significant memories of all four key sub-themes: 43 of all participants could recall their earliest memory, 46 participants covered questions relating to family and identity, 48 on childhood home and standard of living, and 52 on schooling.

The most predominant 'war years' themes featured in the recordings were: the Blitz, which is included in over 94% of interviews (60 participants). The Blitz is followed by memories of rationing (51 participants), and views on the War (39 participants).

Themes that are present in around half of interviews are: evacuation (31) the Americans (27), wartime community (32). The themes that did not feature so comprehensively are: end of the War (22), armed/emergency services (19), POWs (9), wartime politics (7), wartime housing (8) and politics (7).

Within the 'post-war years' theme, over 90% of participants could remember, and had views on, the rebuilding of Plymouth's city centre. Post-war housing and the new estates feature in 34 of the recordings and 26 participants have significant memories on changings in community and social life.

I now highlight some interesting narratives based on key project themes:

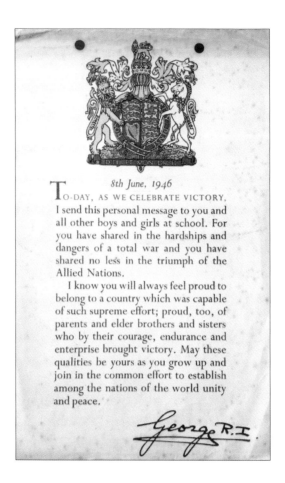

8th June, 1946

TO-DAY, AS WE CELEBRATE VICTORY, I send this personal message to you and all other boys and girls at school. For you have shared in the hardships and dangers of a total war and you have shared no less in the triumph of the Allied Nations.

I know you will always feel proud to belong to a country which was capable of such supreme effort; proud, too, of parents and elder brothers and sisters who by their courage, endurance and enterprise brought victory. May these qualities be yours as you grow up and join in the common effort to establish among the nations of the world unity and peace.

George R.I

At the end of the Second World War
every child in England received a letter from the King.

THE EARLY YEARS

Earliest Memory

As the majority of participants were in their childhood years during the 1940s, not surprisingly, earliest memories for many of them relate to the War.

Air raids and shelters feature strongly within the archive. Vic French recalled his earliest memory:

'My earliest memory is being carried into the air-raid shelter that was in our garden, it was an Anderson shelter. There were two bunk-beds in there, and that's where we went to hide from the air raids.'

Interviewer: 'How did you feel, is it something you remember with fear?'

'Quite neutral feelings, I think at that age there's an absolute reliance on your parents, and the events taking place around you are just the norm.'

Ted Jones described his earliest memory, aged six and a half, of moving between air-raid shelters during an aerial attack.

'In this particular night I was sitting in an air raid shelter with a lot of other people, during a bombing raid by the Germans in Wyndham Square. When an incendiary bomb landed at the back of our air-raid shelter, minutes later an Air Raid Warden told us to leave that shelter and go to one on Wolsdon Street. This was a terrifying experience for all of us because clusters of small incendiary bombs were dropping from the sky as we dodged from one doorway to the next to get to our next air-raid shelter. There was a continuous shattering of glass and the noise of the bombs going off...'

Cousins Joan Wills and Maureen Sawyer recalled:

'The one memory that stands out is we lived in Manor Gardens, which is just off Union Street, and the fires, the bombs, caught all those firms there; furniture, the cinema...and running down past it all to this air-raid shelter, and seeing sailors on the steps of the air-raid shelter that helped us in – to go down the steps.

Family and Identity

When asked about their awareness of social status, it was common within interviewees' replies that an awareness of social class was not obvious, and only occurred occasionally when exposed to other social environments. Valerie Macleod grew up in a wealthy middle-class family in Mannamead, Plymouth. Valerie remembered that she only became aware of her social class when exposed to the opposite end of the social scale on a visit to a local children's home with Lady Astor:

Interviewer: 'Where you aware of your social status?'

'I became aware of it, funnily enough, when I spent a lot of time with Nancy Astor and she took me to visit the Virginia House Settlement where there was a lot of, what I thought, dreadful small children who all had runny noses, ragged clothes and smelt. I had never, until I went out with her, seen that sort of thing, it was foreign to me…social standing is an awful word isn't it…I suppose well-to-do middle-class, is the answer to that.'

Similarly on the other end of the social scale, Ronald Jess grew up in a two-bedroom basement flat in Radnor Place in central Plymouth, and recalled that his neighbourhood had little class consciousness due to a lack of contact with other social status groups:

'There was no class where I lived…well, we knew there was an upper-class but there was no contact with such people…'

David Bacon lived with his parents and maternal grand-parents in a flat in Pembroke Street, Devonport. For him, social status was an alien concept, and was only measured by what essentials some families had over others in his neighbourhood:

'Well it was the slums of Devonport, Pembroke Street, and status…no…that concept didn't mean anything, all I remember is that we weren't as poor as some people there, we had bedding (*laughter*)…'

There were instances however, where interviewees were aware of their family's social status and how this impacted upon their lives. This was most apparent in Barry Tranter's interview, when he discussed his experience of his family moving from being middle to working-class. Barry's father was a senior newspaper editor, but due to his service in the Army he had to take a lower posting after the War. In 1948, when his father acquired a post as a Deputy Sub-Editor at the *Western Morning News,* the family moved from Whitkirk, near Leeds, to 6, Caprera Terrace in Plymouth. Barry recalls:

'We were middle-class, but you can gather I'm no longer middle-class (...) So there we were, we came down from this very nice, modern, three-bedroom, semi-detached house with garage, three garden areas around the house, fields and woods opposite, and suddenly we were living above North Road Station in a...well, basically it was a bedsit with a kitchen and a loft – but accommodation was so desperate in this town you just had to take what you could get, and we had to have somewhere close to the *Western Morning News....*'

THE WAR YEARS, 1939-1945

Many interviewees comment that they were too young at the declaration of War to have any comprehension of what it meant, and their views were formed at a later stage in their lives.

William Jean, who was 3 when War was declared, remarked:

'Well I don't think I felt anything, I was too young to realise the seriousness of it. I probably wouldn't have known what War was....I've only learnt what I've read since, and seen films of, you know...'

Pat Miller commented that it was 'difficult to remember what normal was' as the War was all she knew from an early age. Pat started school the day after the War broke out, at the age of five, and recalled she was taught at school never to admit you were scared, as 'that would make the Germans laugh at you...you weren't upset or frightened, nothing the Germans could do would scare you.'

Some interviewees remember the fear of a German invasion, and how their elders planned to somehow take control of their own destiny, reminding us of the psychological impact this threat had on families across the country. Pat Miller can remember absconding from school during an air-raid and running back home, as her mother said, 'if we're all going to die, we're going to die together.'

Jean Hargraves recalled the lengths her mother may have

been prepared to go to in the event of a German invasion of England:

> 'We had a mantelpiece with a fire, and there was three shilling pieces (on top of the mantelpiece) that you put in the meter, but no one was allowed to touch them. My mum always said that if we were invaded she was going to gas us. So whichever way the War went, we weren't going anywhere, were we! (*chuckles*)... But no, she was determined that the Germans wouldn't get hold of us.'

The Blitz

Between June 1940 and April 1944, Plymouth experienced 602 air raid alerts and 59 bombing raids, which claimed the lives of 1,179 people, and injured a further 3,209. A total of 4,000 properties were destroyed, with a further 18,000 damaged. The city witnessed its worse period of aerial bombing raids between March and April 1941. When France fell to the Nazis, enemy bombers were less than an hour's flight from Plymouth, where the Naval Dockyard, and the presence of the Air Force and Army, made the city a crucial target. (*The Blitz and its Legacy*, Mark Clapson and Peter Larkham, eds. Chap. 12, Stephen Essex and Mark Brayshay). Vivid memories of the Plymouth Blitz live on within many of the project participants, and create a deeply moving narrative of the destruction and loss these individuals witnessed at a young age.

When Muriel Marshall and her twin sister were 20, their family home was in Barclays Chambers in Princess Square,

Plymouth. In March 1941, while she and her family were in the basement, their top-floor flat was destroyed by incendiaries.

Interviewer: 'What do you remember of the Blitz?'

'Well – terrified. I was terrified of being buried, because you heard of people getting buried.'

Interviewer: 'What was is like during the day after the bombing?'

'Oh, it was awful! Some places you'd go...still there... some alms houses at the end of Ebrington Street...I remember passing by and there was bodies lying there as they fell. They couldn't pick them all up at once.'

'All the city centre went. Shops went. Oh, you could smell it, oh..!'

Tom Savery was 8 years old when the bombing started, and explained how he slept for three years in a tunnel at Hooe Quarry. He also described vivid memories of the destruction of the city centre, including the bombing of St Andrew's:

'I remember my mother taking me over to St Andrew's Church and I remember the smouldering, it was still smouldering from the fire that destroyed it.'

Kenneth Bonning, lived in three-storey town house in Devonport when he was a young child, and recalled his feelings or terror he experienced facing air raids on a daily basis:

'It was terrifying. Every night we had to go down...
They'd put an Anderson shelter in our garden, so every
night we had to go down. I crawled out of the shelter
one day and there wasn't much left of the house...and
I remember one night my mother carrying me down
to the shelter and looking up and seeing the search-
lights and spotting a plane – that was probably my
first memory.'

Angela Watts described her near-death experience aged
five, and how certain sounds continue impact upon her
today:

'I lived at St. Budeaux which wasn't very clever,
because we had the railway bridge between Devon
and Cornwall. There was an armament depot up at
Bull Point and there was a big gun up there that was
nicknamed *Big Bertha*. I think most big guns throughout the country were called *Big Bertha*. Why, I don't
remember, but it was. And we lived in Sydney Street
ten years before the war. There was a big block of
council flats built right onto our house, and one night
we were in the air-raid shelter and my stepmother
and I heard *something* coming down, and we knew it
wasn't going to be good. She turned me over onto my
tummy, put her arm across the the bunk and said, 'This
is it Angela, this is the end,' and it was a basket-full of
incendiaries. And of course the flats next door...went,
and the firemen came and played the water-hoses on
our house to save it.'

Interviewer: 'Good grief. Were you scared?'

'Oh yes. Even today thunderstorms and I just don't get on. The noise and the light – to a little girl it was horrible, and I just don't like it now. And every Monday morning, a nuclear siren is tested in the dockyard and it's the same air-raid siren…you know – the wailing up and down?'

Despite the trauma experienced by participants, through the eyes of a child, the effects of War were at times seen as an opportunity for adventure. For example, memories of collecting shrapnel after a bombing raid, is a common memory within the interviews. Jean Hargraves recalled that:

'We used to go out collecting shrapnel in the morning, to see if you could get the biggest bit of shrapnel, you know? Sometimes it was still hot… It was like collecting marbles really.'

Barry Woon described his childhood memories of walking around Plymouth the day after an air-raid:

'We used to go around picking up shrapnel and things like that, see what we could find. You had a job to move around part of the town because the roads were all still covered, until the troops had come along and cleared a lot of the roadways – all piled up. It was terrible really, having known the old Plymouth and then going down and seeing everything gone; Spooners, Woolworths, Marks & Spencers…all of it.'

In addition to collecting shrapnel on his paper round, Fred Brimacombe found an unexploded incendiary bomb near his home:

> 'I actually picked up an incendiary bomb live, over by the Three Crowns pub. It had fallen out of the aircraft I guess, and hit the shooting that come across the front of the house…and that broke its fall as it fell down. 'Course, me like an idiot, goes and picks it up. I had a cousin in the Navy who had just come down from Lowestoft, and I said to him, 'Look at that, that would look good on the mantelpiece.' I picked it up, he said, 'Get rid of that! Chuck it overboard!' (*laughs*)'.

The theme of the sense of adventure found in the city's 'war-scapes' is also obvious in Edward Wilkinson's memories of exploring bombsites in Plymouth:

> 'The bomb-sites were pretty straightforward, if you like, buildings existed – then it was just a pile of rubble, or a skeleton of a building. And there would be a climbing paradise; dangerous today, my God, health and safety would have serious concerns. But touch wood we were okay, we never came to any damage or mischief. There was a bomb shelter in a park near North Hill, which somehow the entrance had got blocked, and I think our mission in life was to unblock this entrance, God knows what we would have found if we did…and with bits of wood and what-have-you 'the gang' tried to get in. I think we succeeded in the end and were very disappointed as there was nothing there apart from it was very damp, and the smell, which was awful… Everyone knew about that (direct hit on Portland Square air-raid shelter), sadly a lot of people died, and

bomb shelters in a way had their own sort of mystique. I know that sound horrific, but as kids we just found this small shelter and thought, 'I wonder what's in there?' You got an affection for bombsites, because it was somewhere to do something and improvise and build dens...'

One of the most graphic and moving narrative was told by Agnes Reynolds, who was 19 years of age when Plymouth received the worse bombing raids in early 1941. Agnes recalled an evening at the cinema with her friend Jean on 21st March 1941, when the hotel next door received a direct hit:

'There was a certain amount of panic because people were evacuating the building...and we could hear planes, and we'd never heard planes like it before. And we got pushed to go out of this door, and of course people were coming down from here and there. You could see the plane flying over...and they were machine-gunning us! My God, we'd never heard machine-gunning. We didn't know what it was. I had hold of Jean, we didn't know what to do...we were paralysed. The next thing, we were standing there shaking, refusing to move forward to go out these doors. We heard a plane coming down, and it was coming down to bomb, and everybody thought, 'My God, they're going to kill us!' And we all fell to the floor, and I swear, we were in six heaps...six, seven, ten deep...and this thing came right over and he dropped a bomb...We all got the splinters from it, but it didn't hit us, it hit next door. But the thing was when it fell, everything fell down on us...glass chandeliers...you can imagine, there were all these glass chandeliers... the ceiling was falling on us and we were still trying to get away from the first bomb...we were horrified. Oh my God! Then of course we picked ourselves up from this, and we were still alive... This is one thing that stuck with me, and it still does, we were hemmed in but they were pushing us to get out...and I looked over sideways and there was this other entrance...and there was this great pile of bodies just like we'd moved from...and there was a white-haired lady on the top... and I thought about her, you know, an old lady. I said, 'Come on Jean, there's an old lady on top, let's help her out.' And I went over to this lady...and I took her arm to help pull her off...and it came off in my hand... she disintegrated. I'd brought an arm out with me... Oh God...they were all dead, every one of them. And if we'd gone out that door, we had gone with them.'

Rationing

In January 1940, the British government introduced food rationing. The scheme was designed to ensure fair shares for all, at a time of national shortage. The Ministry of Food was responsible for overseeing rationing. Every man, woman and child was given a ration book with coupons. These were required before rationed goods could be purchased. Basic foodstuffs such as sugar, meat, fats, bacon and cheese were directly rationed by an allowance of coupons. Certain key commodities were also rationed; petrol in 1939, clothes in June 1941 and soap in February 1942. The end of the war saw additional cuts, and bread began to be rationed in 1946. It was not until the early 1950s that most commodities came 'off the ration'. Meat was the last item to be de-rationed in July 1954.

One way to get rationed items without coupons, usually at greatly inflated prices, was on the black market. Shopkeepers sometimes kept special supplies 'behind the counter', and 'spivs' – petty criminals – traded in goods often obtained by dubious means. By March 1941, 2,300 people had been prosecuted and severely penalised for fraud and dishonesty. (Source: Imperial War Museum: http://www.iwm.org.uk/history/rationing-in-the-second-world-war)

There is little evidence in the interviews of the black market, although it is mentioned in Jean Hargraves' recording:

> 'Oh yes, I think my mother was part of it (the black market). We did pretty well actually...she's dead now, so you can't touch her (*chuckles*)...she had five children to feed.'

Despite food restrictions, people recall a certain amount of self-sufficiency. This was not only 'digging for victory' in the garden, but also taking advantage of Plymouth's coastal location. David Bacon recounted:

> 'Fish, (there was) plenty. When the mackerel was in, we'd gorge ourselves on that. I very often caught a fish for a meal. Mutton Cove at Devonport, you couldn't squeeze another person in there, and the place was lined with men catching fish.'

Edward Luscombe remembered that his school had been given a field:

'In 1942 the school had been given use of a field in Compton. The idea being to turn it into allotments, and each of us at the school was encouraged to have a piece of this field to grow vegetables.'

Pat Miller provided a comprehensive narrative of her memories of rationing, including the resourcefulness of her neighbourhood (at Hooe) in sharing and recycling food:

'You had a ration book and you had to go to a certain grocer's shop that you were licensed to go to. If eggs were rationed one week and you got a bad egg, you had to take it back, and chances were you wouldn't get a fresh egg in replacement as there wasn't enough to go around... My mother got a bar a soap before the War and that lasted us *all* the War. You never left your tablet of soap on the basin, like they do these days, you kept it in a saucer and used every little bit. You'd never leave any food. You'd scrape up all the crumbs, I don't remember ever being hungry, *ever*, because my mother was a good cook and a good manager. You were severely limited on what you could have, but it was a well-balanced diet, as far as I could tell. You'd grow your own fruit and vegetables and you'd share any surplus with neighbours, or neighbours who had hens would swap a few eggs for a few cabbages... And there was a swill bin outside the houses and the scraps would then go to feed the pigs. So we used to recycle, and we'd never waste anything, it was criminal to waste anything.'

Pat also recalled how her family were helped by relatives in America:

'Clothes were rationed, and it was very difficult to find clothes, especially for growing children, but I was very lucky because we had relatives in America, and they used to send us over clothes, so as a little girl I was very well dressed.'

Some participants can remember their family 'bargaining' and swapping coupons, for example, Arthur Rugg recalled:

'...there used to be lots of bargaining in those days. Me, my mum and my dad didn't have a sweet tooth so all our sweet ration coupons went to other people and they would give us things in return for that.'

As many of the participants were just children during the war, memories of sweet-rationing feature quite strongly in interviews. Barry Woon recalled how he would substitute sweets:

'We were only concerned about our sweets, I suppose. And you couldn't get very many; the shop wouldn't lend it. I think it was about '47 when *Cadbury's Dairy Milk* came in...but we used to get...I think they were called *Horlicks* or *Ovaltine*...tablets which, if you'd used your ration, you could use these as sweets, you'd go to Boots, or somewhere like that, to buy them.'

Tom Savery remembered the excitement he felt when sweet-rationing ended and his wonderment at the introduction of exotic fruit, such as bananas, now being more widely available in the UK:

> 'You were allowed to buy three pennies-worth of sweets a week, I think, and I remember, in '48 I think it was, after the War, sweets were de-rationed, and as a kid I couldn't conceive of going into a shop and to have as much as you wanted...and there was something called a 'banana' we'd read about in books, but we'd never seen a banana you see...we'd seen monkeys eating them in the *Mowgli* stories, but we never had bananas during the War.'

Evacuation

Barry Woon was evacuated to Penzance along with his peers at his school in Peverell. He recalled the first six weeks that he spent in a workhouse:

> 'Yes the whole school was evacuated, one of the...well, you look back on it now and I suppose it was funny... the house I was in, which was Grenville House, we were all put in the workhouse with some of the inmates still there – in the workhouse! We had no beds, but had mattresses on the floor...'

Nonetheless, Barry remembers this time with affection for, 'as young lads it was of course a big laugh, and there were fields there we could play cricket...'

Being evacuated from the city did not always mean safety

from the conflict however, as Barry recalls, after being moved from the workhouse, he and his fellow evacuees were spread around hotels in the Penzance area, and one of the buildings got bombed:

> '...they had the Hotel Royale, the Chy-an-Dour which was a big house, and several other hotels that they took over, but not long after we got down there – we left Plymouth from the Blitz – the house that some of the crowd of boys was in was bombed, the only thing that was actually killed was the house-masters dog...'

Jean Hargraves described how the farm near Redruth where she was evacuated, was also bombed:

> 'The worst part of my life throughout the war was being sent down to Redruth as an evacuee. Me and my sister, she was six years older than me, so we were put on a farm and this farmer had four daughters. Now he needed two more. Anyway, they were very good with us, I'm not saying anything about them... but we had to go in to where they make the butter and it was freezing. Back home we had a hammock (in the shelter) with all mod cons around, so I wasn't very happy there at all. After about two and a half to three weeks, a landmine was dropped right near the farm house. Really bad, killed cows.'

Far from feeling safe, Jean recalls evacuation as feeling far from contented, and after three weeks, shortly after the bombing of the farm, Jean and her sister retuned to Plymouth at her mother's request.

For some individuals the experience of evacuation was temporary and spasmodic, such as Colin Baser, who was evacuated with his mother and siblings to numerous places in Devon and Cornwall:

> 'Well, during the Blitz…we always seemed to be moving around. Now for some reason we'd find ourselves…the three of us and Mother – not Father –I can remember us going out to country cottages and we'd stay a night, or two nights, and at one stage we were evacuated to St. Austell where we were billeted with the Mitchell family… An anecdote I always tell people about the War is that sometimes we were bundled in lorries and taken to church halls where we'd stay the night as a family, Mother and the three of us, and we stayed in a church. The church that we stayed at, I found out after the war, was at Yelverton, which was right next to Harrowbeer Airport that was being used by American planes, which is a strange place to take people out to during the war.'

Pat Miller was evacuated from Plymouth due to her father's posting at RAF Culdrose. Far from being made to feel welcome, Pat recalled feelings of isolation as an 'outsider', for example, when queuing at a shop for doughnuts in Newquay, the assistant refused to give her a doughnut as she was a 'vacee' (evacuee).

After her house was bombed, Betty Buzza's family moved from Plymouth to Gateshead to stay with in-laws. Gateshead was still a target for aerial attacks however, and proved to be a traumatic experience for Betty:

'…we lived up there for about four years, and while I was there, every time the sirens sounded, I used to scream and scream, you know? So Welfare put me in this convalescence home in a place called Silloth, just on the outskirts of Scotland, yes, so I was there and my mother used to come weekends to see me.'

Americans

In key with many oral histories recorded across Britain, many memories of American Servicemen relate to receiving free gifts of food and the rapid departure of troops before D-Day.

Ted Jones recalled visiting the American base at Marsh Mills:

'We used to have a big Army camp down in Marsh Mills, all the yanks there, you know? We used to go down there, as kids, and they used to give us chewing-gum and all that. On occasions my older brother would go down there and get the odd tin of SPAM.' *(chuckles)*

Barry Woon remembers getting chewing-gum off American and Polish servicemen:

'Yes Americans and Poles, there were quite a few Polish sailors over here, they had a few ships and they managed to get away, but Americans, yes there were quite a few Americans here before D-Day, and we could get chewing-gum and things like that from them.'

Angela Watts remembered being given sweets through

the railings of her school playground:

> The Americans had sweets, we didn't. And I'd walk to school, and up over Crownhill there was a big group of Americans stationed there, and they used to pass sweets through the railings to us children. Yes. Of course you were *made* if you had some sweets, not just one or two, but *bags* of them...'

A less happy memory for Angela was witnessing the troops walk past her home in St Budeaux in preparation for D-Day:

> 'Yes. I can remember seeing them walk down past the bungalow, to go off for D-Day and some of the poor dear gents were crying. I've often wondered how many that I personally saw, survived. That's why it's called Normandy Way at St. Budeaux...beside the bridge there was a little step-way and that's where they went from. There are some plaques down there to say, 'This is where the Americans embarked for D-Day.'

Audrey Uglow recalled how her family would entertain American troops in their home:

> 'When the Americans came to prepare for D-Day there were some of them stationed out at Eggbuckland Keep and some at Mount Wise. Anyway, so we used to have the Americans home to our bungalow quite a bit because they were missing home. We didn't actually know D-Day was coming, but we sensed the fact, and knew that probably next week or the week after they weren't going to be here. We did hear from some of

them afterwards, but some of them that we knew, didn't survive.'

Tom Savery, who grew up in Hooe, described his memories is the run-up to D-Day:

'Over at Hooe, I remember the American soldiers that came across and took over. I remember just before D-Day, the Sound was absolutely jam-packed with craft. You could almost walk from Jennycliff to Mount Edgcumbe on the boats. Absolutely jam-packed. And a day of so after D-Day I went up there with my parents and it was empty, *everything* had gone. *All* the craft had gone.'

Memories of white and black segregation are not common in the recordings. Pat Miller however, recalled the American camp at Radford Wood, Plymstock. She remembered the segregation between white and black Americans, and that only white Americans were allowed to drink in local pubs. She commented that people in Britain were very 'naive' at that time, and many had never seen a black man before. In her village of Hooe however, she witnessed no prejudice towards the black troops from the inhabitants, '...as it was War and we were all in it together.'

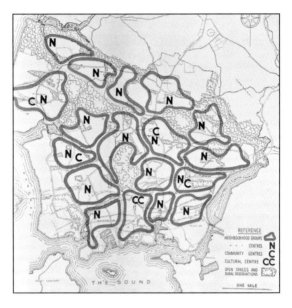

'To regain the community spirit of neighbourliness is essential if civic consciousness is to be preserved. Here are shown in cartoon form the various areas in the city which by reason of topography and natural trend might form the basis of neighbourhood grouping; each group a compact self-contained entity.'

A suggested plan for neighbourhood groups
from *A Plan For Plymouth*, 1943

THE POST-WAR HOUSING PERIOD, 1945-1955

At the heart of Plymouth's reconstruction plans were a tiny group of influential participants, who had set out all of its key principles within just seven months of the worst of the raids. The group comprised of Lord Astor (the City's Mayor), Lord Reith (Minister of Works and Buildings), and Patrick Abercrombie (Consultant Planner). Abercrombie worked on the Plan for Plymouth with James Paton Watson (the City's Engineer and Surveyor), who rapidly embraced its radical ideas and become key figure in its implementation. (*The Blitz and its legacy*, Mark Clapson and Peter Larkham, eds. Chap. 12, Stephen Essex and Mark Brayshay, pp. 153-155)

Views on the Abercrombie/Paton Watson Plan for Plymouth

Memories of '*A Plan for Plymouth*' (1943) featured predominately in the interviews. Although the Plan bears a publication date of 1943, it was not approved by the City Council until 25th April, 1944. It was at this point that the full details become more widely known, with copies being available at a subsidised price of 10s 6d (ten and six), approx. 53p. (Clapson/Larkham, 155). Many participants recall their excitement at looking at the document, such as Pat Miller, who recalled looking at the family copy of '*A Plan for Plymouth*', and thinking that such a 'wonderful vision could never come to fruition from all the rubble,' and her amazement at new department stores in Plymouth, as she 'had never seen anything like it before.'

Others memories of the Plan however, were often tinged with disappointment when the rebuilding was being executed. Edward Luscombe, for example, still has a copy of the document which he discussed in his interview. He recalled that he found it 'a very exciting book', and looked forward to the rebuilding but how, due to a lack of funds, many of the exciting parts of the plan never came to fruition.

Barry Woon expressed that the new city centre doesn't have the same character that pre-war Plymouth had, and thought the rebuilding took too long, and remembers some places not being built on until forty years after the War.

A juxtaposition of views on the reconstruction was common in many participant narratives. For example, Kenneth Bonning described his disproval of many factors of the Abercrombie Plan, including the destruction of many old buildings that had survived the War and the introduction of the 'Americanised road system' in which streets were laid out in a grid pattern:

> 'Well they knocked down some nice places, didn't they? We went into the Corn Exchange to see a chap called '*Syncopating Sandy*' play when we were boys, and things *happened* in Plymouth. But then all of sudden they knocked it down and tried to make it all square, like America, which was a bit sad really, they should have kept all the nice buildings of Plymouth. They knocked stuff down unnecessarily I think…they took the Guinness Clock away, didn't they? Cut Ebrington Street in half, Bedford Street was a nice street, but it all

had to go, and I don't understand why, even the old Pannier market was attractive.'

Nevertheless he recalls his childhood wonderment about innovative new technology he saw appearing around him in the rebuilding of the city:

'It was nice to see it, I remember the first escalator, it was in Dingles, and we rode up and down that thirty or forty times (*chuckles*). I mean, new technology was coming along all the time. My chum, the chap who lived next door to us on Gordon Terrace, he came out of the Navy and joined the Corporation as a steam-roller driver. He had a big steam-roller he drove up and down…and I used to sit up there with him…and that's what it meant to me, that things were changing and innovation was coming in, and to see all the glass and all the rest of the nonsense that was coming in. Rationing was finishing…they were knocking down buildings putting up new ones…it was all innovation really.'

Post-war housing and the new estates

The Plymouth Blitz and other *Luftwaffe* bombing raids during World War II saw 3,754 homes destroyed and 8,000 damaged, leaving the city with an acute housing problem. As in all of Britain's cities, one answer came in the form of 'temporary' prefabricated concrete homes. Each took as little as four days to build, but proved so sturdy that many survive today.

Muriel Marshall recalled the fondness that many people

felt towards prefabs in Plymouth, and suggests how some individuals felt distraught when they had to move out to new housing:

'The American prefabs had come over, and they were only supposed to last around 14 years; well they lasted a lot longer. People were whispering something, and do you know what they were saying? 'They've got a *fridge!*' (Before then) no British people had a fridge, and they had central heating...and all the roads had American names, Michigan Way, Oregon Way... Oh, people loved them, they were cosy in comparison – all mod cons. A lot of the people cried their hearts out...one woman I knew, they sent her to Southway, she didn't like it, and asked if she could have another change, she never really settled down there...'

During the late 1940s and 1950s, new council house estates were built at Efford, Ham, Honicknowle, Kings Tamerton, Ernesettle and Whitleigh. From 1951-1957, around 1,000 new council homes were built each year as the city expanded northwards.

✝ Ted Jones' family moved to Efford during the 1950s. His narrative presents a positive picture of post-war estates in Plymouth:

'We moved in 1952 to Kirton Place in Efford. It was a nice two-bedroom house and we had a huge back garden, so big we grew vegetables. In fact we grew so much we were supplying our neighbours with it because we could never eat it all. The neighbourhood community stayed together for many years, not like today when you don't know your neighbours…you could go out and leave your front door open, go up the shop, come back, nothing would've happened to it.'

Arthur Rugg also recalls the new estate of Efford as being a safe and green place to be, with a good sense of community. Arthur's family were not rehoused after the War and continued to live in their flat in Embankment Road. He recalled his mother being envious of his aunt and uncle for being given a new council house at Efford:

Interviewer: 'At the end of the war you were still living in that house? You didn't move to one of the new areas?'

'No we hoped we would be able to – my mum was very upset because my Aunt Aida had come to live in the house as well, and she had three children, and they were given a council house out at Efford estate and it was full of orchards and all kinds of things. They had just started to build the estate, only two roads were being built at that point and my aunt and uncle got the first house in the road. We used to go there and visit them. It was a fantastic house with all the facilities…'

Arthur's narrative also demonstrates how rural the new estates, such as Efford, were considered to be at this time, in comparison to the inner city:

'We children used to run off and play in the fields and things, where we got chased by the farmer because we were pinching apples. You'd feel you were out in the countryside as there was virtually no building there.'

New council housing also occurred in Devonport, clearing poor areas of the pre-war era. David Bacon's kin were one of the families to be rehoused from the Devonport 'slums' after the War, he remembers:

> 'They were clearing Pembroke Street, a slum clearance thing, and moving people into council flats or houses, a lot of them went out to Swilly. We moved into a four-bedroomed flat in Clarence Street.'

Interviewer: 'and what was that like?'

> 'Heaven! Absolute heaven! If you think about it, (before) there was Mum, Dad when he was there, three boys and a girl all in one room. And to have a bathroom – that was luxury! By modern standards you'd probably consider it to be a bit spartan, but it was heaven for us.'

Despite David's wonderment at the mod cons of his new family home, later in his interview he mentioned that he did not have so many friends in the Clarence Street flats, and that people 'kept themselves to themselves more...' This reminds us that far from the healthy and happy communities present in the utopian vision of modernist town planning, many people experienced isolation, and in extreme cases depression, when rehoused in edge-of-town estates and inner-city tower blocks.

George Easton moved into a prefab in Lipson Vale with his wife and daughter, but his description of his new home was not so cosy as in Muriel Marshall's description of prefabs, and he recalls the damp conditions caused in part by a leaking wall. His family were later given a three-bed council house in Efford, and despite being pleased with the affordability helped by the introduction of housing benefit, he felt that Efford had 'no community'.

There are examples of some individuals who, despite moving to new estates, continued to connect to their 'old communities.' After the War, Edward Luscombe's family were relocated in a 'steel house' in the new estate of West Park. Interestingly, for his family, St Gabriel's Church in Peverell, now over two miles away, is where their mainstay of community remained, and the family did not feel engaged in their new community to any great extent:

> 'Well, when we moved to this steel house I was very much attached to going to church, and very much involved in St Gabriel's. I think one of the things that annoyed me was instead of being about two-hundred yards from the Church I was now about two and a half miles, which was a bind as far as I was concerned. I went to church on the bus or I cycled… Occasionally I would go to St Francis, Honicknowle. See, in those days it was quite common to go to church and communion service fasting… I used to be in Passion plays, Nativity plays, youth club activities and all that…'

Interviewer: 'Did some sort of community build up around your home in West Park?'

'I think so yes, but I wouldn't say for me, or for us, because that was the other side of the valley, the community that we were attached was St Francis, Honicknowle, we got involved in that a bit, but as my attachment was to St Gabriel I didn't really get too involved in Honicknowle.'

Edward's narrative suggests that factors, such as religious community, were more powerful than spatial surroundings, and the more 'manufactured' society of post-war estates were often overridden by pre-existing emotional or spiritual 'communities'.

* * *

A PLAN FOR PLYMOUTH

THE REPORT PREPARED FOR THE

CITY COUNCIL

by

J. PATON WATSON, M.INST.C.E., M.INST.M.&CY.E.

City Engineer and Surveyor

and

PATRICK ABERCROMBIE, M.A., F.R.I.B.A., P.P.T.P.I.

Consultant

WITH APPENDICES ON AGRICULTURE AND SOIL

by

DUDLEY STAMP, D.SC., and G. W. ROBINSON, M.A., SC.D.

INTRODUCTION BY

The Lord Mayor of Plymouth

THE RIGHT HON. THE VISCOUNT ASTOR

WITH A FOREWORD BY

His Excellency the American Ambassador to the Court of St. James,

THE HON. JOHN G. WINANT

UNDERHILL, (PLYMOUTH), LTD.,

REGENT STREET, PLYMOUTH, ENGLAND

1943

Interview Extracts

PARTICIPANTS
(first name alphabetical order)

Agnes Reynolds, born 18th August 1921, in Alexander Road, Mutley, Plymouth:

I was 18 in August 1939, and we went to war in the September. I'd had a wonderful holiday at Bovisand with my sister and the whole fort was full of Territorials (Army Reserve), looking after it, and training there. They used to put a flag out to sea to say they were practising. Of course these were young men, and we used to go swimming with them, down over the cliffs…it was lovely! It was such fun but I never thought *you may go out and get killed lad, how much life have you got left?* It didn't really dawn on me, and I'm quite a forward-thinking person, it was only when I found out that my brother was going to war…

We had a habit of going to the pictures together, me and my girl-friend. We both were great dancers, and were like sisters, and she was how I would have loved to have been. She was tiny and pretty. Natural blonde hair, lovely features, great chest and body on her, and she could swim – lovely legs – gorgeous-looking girl. I never envied her – don't think that – but I did think, *I wish I had all that.* I was slim, it's true enough, but I had straight dark brown hair with a fringe, and looked very ordinary I used to think, when we were talking to boys whose eyes were not on me, but on little Jean. It sounds like envy, but it wasn't – I loved her, loved her dearly, and she was a beautiful dancer – we used to giggle together, oh she was sweet. When we went dancing with boys there was no touching below the waist, and you could go swimming with them but you never had any boy touch you inappropriately, it wasn't done in those days.

Me and Jean knew each day what we were going to do that night. She and her father worked in the Customs and Excise down on the Barbican and I was working at a timber firm at that time, it was the first job I got – seven and sixpence a week – and I had to do the typing. I was lucky to get it, with the education and everything. Fifteen times I'd applied for a job and this was the only one I'd got a reply to – it was my handwriting – they used to compliment me on my handwriting. So I said, 'We're going to the pictures tonight!' and the film was Mickey Rooney in *Strike up the Band*. Real noisy film, lovely – we thought Mickey Rooney was wonderful – and it was a lovely modern cinema down there with a beautiful frontage, and when you went in there was these big curved stairs up to the circle, you see, and big gates to go into the main screen, but we always went downstairs, we never bothered to go upstairs because downstairs was such a huge area and when you were vacating the place – if you'd been upstairs – you'd have to wait ages to get out through the main doors. They used to charge us sixpence, or a shilling a night each, but little Jean didn't have the money. I said, 'I'll pay for you this time – come on we'll go!' So, we got in. I can see her now, she was so lovely and you know, I want to make this statement: when I love someone, I love them dearly and I loved her so much. I can't love in a small way – I love in a big way...so this brings me back to a sad time.

We both got in and got seats. We didn't want to be too far back, but in the middle. We got nice seats there and we were sat with our carton of sweets and everybody was waiting for *Strike up the Band* to start and all the big news... Because it was such a loud film we didn't really hear the siren – it was muffled by the strength of volume in the room. There was some restlessness going on... and then we saw the manager running along the front of the screen and everybody got a bit worried. Then we could hear something going on outside – you could hear planes... The manager eventually had to turn the picture off. He came up to the front and he said, 'I'm afraid it's getting a little hot outside – I'll have to ask you to vacate the cinema. Please go quietly.' We were downstairs and it was all dark, we were fumbling getting out. Back then there were huge double doors out onto the street and also two smaller side doors, so most people would go through the big doors, but we came straight out. There was a certain amount of panic in vacating, and we could hear the planes but we'd never heard planes like this before in our lives. We came out of this middle door and got pushed out onto the street, and we couldn't believe it – we'd come out of the darkness and here all this was going on. We could see the planes flying overhead and they were actually machine-gunning us, and my God we'd never heard machine-gunning in our lives – we weren't even sure what it was. I was in front of Jean and there were about two people in front of me with a big crowd behind, and I had hold of Jean, and we were real scared, we didn't know what to do... What do you do in these circumstances? We didn't know – we were paralysed. We were standing there shaking, the pair of us, refusing to move forward to go any further because we didn't know what was going on. Then we heard the smash of something that had come down and landed in the shops, there was this *whooof* sound, a bomb had gone off and there was this smell of fire and I don't think we could move. Then, still terrified because we'd heard that bomb nearby, we heard a plane coming back very close and everybody thought *Oh my God – they're coming to kill us* and we all fell to the floor. I swear we were in…six heaps… with everyone who had come down the staircase too, and we got right down to the floor, everybody on top of one another – six, seven, ten deep – and I got separated from Jean. This plane came right over us and he dropped a bomb on the hotel that was attached to the cinema. We heard it and then we were covered in glass and splinters – but it didn't hit us – it hit next door. Everything fell down on us…glass, chandeliers…you can imagine…the ceiling was falling on us and we were still trying to get away from the first bomb…we were horrified. Oh my God. Then we picked ourselves up from this, we were still alive but I had to find Jean under all these people, 'Jean! Jean, where are you Jean?' then I saw her blonde hair and I picked her up. She said, 'What are we going to do?' and I said, 'I don't know, dear – we've got to get out of here, but we can't go out there again!' Everybody was asking stupid questions and – this still sticks with me – we were hemmed in by the exit and people were pushing us to get out, so everyone put their backs together to hold the mass behind. I looked over, sideways, and there was this other entrance with a great pile of bodies, just like the one we'd come from, and there was a white-haired lady on the top. I was standing there holding on, everybody was, where could we go? We were all one mass together, but nobody felt safe. We didn't know whether to move left or right, and I was thinking about this woman, 'Come on Jean, there's a lady on the top – let's help her out.' We went across to this lady – she was laying on top of the heap looking this way. I took her arm to help pull her off…and it came off in my hand. She disintegrated. I brought an arm out with me. Oh God almighty – they were all dead, every single one of them. And if we'd gone out that door we'd have been with them.

That's when the shock hit me. *Holy Mother of God* – I used to say the Hail Mary then – *Oh Mother of God* – she must have saved me. Then everybody noticed this pile of people, but everyone was leaving them there in a hump – well, what do you do with them? All I saw was the white-haired lady…it stuck with me for years, the sight of that, and I was only 18. It was an awful shock and Jean, my little friend, was petrified. We had to get out of this and it was about an hour that they were dropping bombs and flying up and down the roads machine-gunning us. We didn't have a clue, we had no idea, we had nothing… We weren't even able to save Plymouth from the fire – we thought we had everything we needed, but we didn't have the water even though the sea was *right* beside us. It was bombed to a cinder…that was a time when you grew up.

I'd seen dead people, it wasn't anything new because in my home we'd had two grandmas who'd lived with us and died. You see them, living in a Catholic house. I'd lost my little baby sister when she was 11 months old, she was like a little china doll, and Grandma was about 68 when she died, and I'd go up to the bedroom and she'd been laid out in the bed so I had seen it, but I'd never met up with it to touch, and I think the pulling out of that arm was… I just couldn't imagine what was happening…but it was something dreadful. Nobody touched this pile, what could we do? I couldn't pull her off; I had to leave her there. It was still going on but had eased a bit after a while, and we weren't hearing machine-gunning anymore. I saw a small door open, and a couple of men go through to outside, sticking close to the wall. I said, 'Come on Jean, we must get out in case they bomb this place again.' We stayed this side of the wall, and followed others who were going in to this building next door – it was The Royal Hotel public house. People there were taking the bottles and swigging from them…I found a little corner, and said, 'Jean, let's sit down here and I'll pray.' So I sat there and started saying my prayers to the Blessed Virgin. She said, 'Well, I *can't* pray!' you see, she had no religion. So I said, 'Never mind! Just listen to me!' I was saying *Our Fathers* and *Hail Marys* and still listening…because you could hear it all the time, those that flew over machine-gunning were the ones that scared the life out of me. People were getting drunk around us and people were stealing things and it frightened us to see these young men, these sailors…one fella came over slurring, 'I'll look after you…' No thank you.

I *never* expected to come home. Never. I thought *well this is where I'm going to die* but the thing that worried me was that we'd gone into a *pub*, snuggled up together in the cellar of this place where alcohol was kept, and I thought *if anything happens to me and Father finds out where my body was found*...because we were in a hotel that had prostitutes! You could pick up a girl and go to a room there any day... and my father would think *My God, what was she doing there?* I remember thinking this! *What will Daddy think that I was doing in* The Royal, *when I told him I was going to the pictures?* Silly thought, but it was so real to me at that age.

Anyway, eventually it was quiet. There was an elderly couple near me, so I said, 'What do you think it's like?' 'How far do you have to go?' they said. 'We've got to get to Mutley, but I don't know how we're going to get there' I said. He said, 'I dare say we'll all find it difficult, dear, but I'm gonna take my wife, and try it now - while it seems quiet.' So we followed him out this door. By this time, the manager had come down to tell us it was no good sheltering there, because the whole hotel was on fire, so we got out. It was quieter, you couldn't hear them any more, just the noise of the burning and the stench, people flying around crazy, screaming and shouting for each other, but...where to go? I could not even find a road to follow. The whole lot was flat as a pancake in front of us. I didn't know whether to go left, front or centre. We had on nice little shoes, and there was rubble and dust... the houses, things standing up, you're looking in amazement, where there used to be a road...then we saw Derry's Clock, it was still there! So I said we'd make our way towards it. We were holding hands walking up there to go to Royal Parade but it wasn't the road, I didn't know whether we were in Cornwall Street, I know it wasn't Old Town Street, we didn't know which way we were going, we just held onto each other and walked in that direction.

we had to go North, that would be home that way, so we carried on up through there and there were other people picking their way, coming out from where they'd been in the cinema, so it was getting full of people and I wanted to get away from them to see where I was going. There were parts of buildings...and you didn't want them to collapse...so you're trying to keep to the middle of the place but it was full of what had been either side of it.

We got up to Drake Circus and I said to go up the side that wasn't as busy. Sometimes we'd hear a crash of something that would fall down...I don't think I'd ever had terror like it in my life, and never will again, and I felt so responsible for Jean because she was an only child and I thought if anything happened to her they hadn't got any other children – and *I'd* asked her to go. She hadn't any money and *I'd* said, 'I'll pay for you.' I was thinking of me getting home and telling her mum and dad she'd died... the funny thoughts...*if anything happens to Jean, I hope I go with her, because I don't want to tell anybody she's died.* All the mad thoughts I had there.

Thinking back, it was a rude awakening for us – how many people face machine-guns unless you're like we were? It's all right if you're a soldier - but we'd never seen violence. In this part of the world we don't even have earthquakes! We get a lot of rain, but have a very simple life. We're very lucky to live in this country, I love England. I love my country, I do really, I'm very proud of it, really and truly. I don't care what other people think.

Angela Watts, née Tonkin, born August 1935, in Penzance:

Interviewer: Can you give me your earliest memory?

Yes, certainly. In Penzance there's a lovely garden called Morrab Gardens and as a little two-year-old girl I was intrigued by the fountain there. I was always dressed in cream...cream skirt, cream coat, cream hat – Panama hat – and that day it had been raining. You can imagine what I'm going to say? I ran around the fountain and fell down in to the mud...and my lovely cream outfit was ruined.

Later we lived at St. Budeaux, which wasn't very clever, because we were by the railway bridge between Devon and Cornwall. There was an armament depot up at Bull Point, and there was a big gun up there that was nick-named 'Big Bertha'. I think most big guns throughout the country were called Big Bertha. Why, I don't remember but it was. And we lived in Sydney Street ten years before the war. There was a big block of council flats built right onto our house and one night, when I was five years old, we were in the air-raid shelter and my stepmother and I heard *something* coming down – we knew it wasn't going to be good. She turned me over onto my tummy, put her arm across the bench and the bunk and said, 'This is it Angela, this is the end!' and it was a basket full of incendiaries coming down! The flats next door, they went, and the firemen came and played the water hoses on our house to save it.

Interviewer: Do you remember feeling scared?

Oh yes. Even today thunderstorms and I just don't get on. The noise and the light – to a little girl it was horrible and I still don't like it now. And every Monday morning, there's a nuclear siren tested in our Dockyard and it's the same air-raid siren…you know, the wailing up and down? And I hear that if I'm out and in the garden…you jump. Ingrained isn't it?

I can remember being in the school at Victoria Road in St. Budeaux and there was an air raid and we were watching them all – the planes – fighting. Another time we were in our garden, it was during the night and the Germans were coming over and one was shot down. I don't know whether it was by Big Bertha or not, but we all cheered.

Interviewer: Were you aware that something had changed?

Yes. Yes you were very aware that…we took more precaution about things, about lights for example. The house I lived in with my grandparents only had gas-lamps downstairs, and the bedrooms were upstairs so you had to go up with a candle, and the candle flickered, and that was always creepy. And going back into the house after an air-raid, I hated it. I was always afraid there was a German there, waiting for me. How he got into the house and waiting for me I've no idea! But again…to a child's mind…

Interviewer: Tell me about the clothes you used to wear?

I can remember my stepmother, she knitted a lot, and she knitted me a dress, or probably dresses. And knitted bathing costumes. And you went into the water and they'd be down *here*! Ghastly things, absolutely ghastly.

Yes. But I can see Dad now on the beach with his shoes and his tie and his jacket...we wouldn't dream of going onto a beach like that nowadays, would we?

Interviewer: So, tell me about Plymouth being bombed?

Yes, after the episode in St Budeaux when the basket of incendiaries came down, the next day we went to Slapton and stayed for about six months – that was where my stepmother came from. That night they woke me up to show me the glow of Plymouth burning. In the sky you could see it was all red. Her family were farmers and I enjoyed being on the farm. We had *cream*! We used to walk down to the beach, in the summer, and they had a dog called Kipper and they used to have a hotel on the beach at Slapton, sadly Kipper got onto a mined area of the beach and he was blown up. I wasn't there on that particular day, thank goodness. You know where Torcross is? There's a hotel there that has a picture of that hotel on the beach, and it also tells about how 'Kipper Luscombe' got onto the mines. My stepmother's family never went back to their farm afterwards – they'd been ordered to leave before the practices for D-Day.

I had a friend who was born and bred on the Barbican and she was older than me...so she would have been going out with her boyfriend...I think it was her husband. They went to the pictures one evening and they walked home past St Andrews church which had been bombed, and was on fire, and they were stood there in awe of seeing St. Andrews in flames. I mean, whoever would have thought it, you know? They stood there for five minutes and they suddenly realised, 'We shouldn't be standing around here!' so they ran home. The firemen came and played their water hoses onto the bell-ropes, so that they saved the bells – they suddenly thought they could do that if they couldn't save the rest of the church. There are some photographs inside the church of Lady Astor in the ruins the day after, so do go in and see them.

Interviewer: A lot of people I've spoken to remember the Americans that came here?

Yes. The Americans had sweets and we didn't. I'd walk to school – up over to Crownhill – and there was a big group of Americans stationed up there, and they used to pass sweets through the railings to us children! Of course you were *made* if you had some sweets – not just one or two – but *bags* of them! We had our sports day up on Bowden Park Road, and I remember walking home and all of us children had our names on a little tags on our clothes, you know? I was walking past the barracks and this American voice said, 'Hello Angela Tonkin!' I said, '*How* do you know my *name*?' 'Well, it says it on your badge!' he said.

I can remember seeing them walk down past our bungalow to go off for D-Day and some of the poor, dear gents were crying. I've often wondered how many that I personally saw survived. That's why it's called Normandy Way, at St. Budeaux, did you realise? Yes, that was the way they went, the bit down to the bridge – there was a little step-way there and that's where they went from. There are some plaques down there to say that this is where the Americans embarked for D-Day.

Angela Watts in St Andrew's Church, Plymouth

Portrait by Fotonow

Anthony Richard Kingdom, born 1931, family from Cornwall and Devon:

My next-door neighbour was Gordon Hancock and he went to Froebel House School, Stoke. Before I recount one of my most traumatic memories of air-raids on Plymouth, I must explain that as a nine-year-old I ran with Gordon and his three friends, who were all at least four years older than me, therefore exploits I encountered were often those of thirteen and fourteen-year-old boys. They were in my neighbourhood, and there were no children my own age, so much to their reluctance, Gordon and his friends had to put up with me tagging along. I can remember Gordon and I finding live rounds of ammunition. At one time, we found a complete incendiary bomb, which has gone into a bucket. We tried our hardest to set it alight and hammer it and that, but it wouldn't burn! It just wouldn't burn!

One night RAF pilots shot down a plane over the city and it was on fire, spiralling down out of control coming straight for our area. It transpired later the next day that one of its propeller blades fell on the roof of the house of Mr Rice, adjacent to us, and ripped off his guttering and damaged slates. I remember pulling the door and curtain shut and waiting for the inevitable crash, possibly right on our house, but it veered off in a westerly direction and crashed on Froebel House School, now the site of New Zealand House, at the junction of Rainham Road and Penlee Way. The blaze lit up the sky and when the raid was finally over wardens came around with loud-speakers as the All Clear was sounding, telling us to remain in our shelters because the exploding ammunition was still going off from the burning aircraft and the possibility of getting accidentally shot by stray bullets travelling at a low trajectory was very real. A wide-open space of some several acres, forming Penlee allotments, was all that was between us and the burning aircraft. Peering out of the shelter and the lee of the house, we could see and hear the exploding ammunition and its tracers flying overhead, some very low indeed. Eventually in the early hours of the morning we were allowed back in our houses and apart from the dull glow in the sky all remained normal. Unfortunately, for Gordon and me, it did not end there, for the craze of all schoolboys of the time was to collect shrapnel and souvenirs of war, of all sorts.

Anthony, aged seven, a pupil at Smeaton College Prep School on the Hoe, before it was destroyed during the Blitz.

Early next morning we decided to find the aircraft and to obtain some pieces for souvenirs. Knowing the Home Guard wardens and the police would be out in force cordoning off all approaches to the site, we decided the only way to gain any access would be the hard way around – going up through the allotments. This we did and appeared inside the cordoned off area, coming out of the top of Rainham Road. In those days a public footpath ran from this point all the way to the bus depot at Milehouse, and also at that point stood several large trees, possibly oaks. The area was deserted and we noticed that the trees were fairly badly damaged – branches and splintered wood everywhere. On closer inspection, we discovered one of the engines of the plane had broken away and crashed into these trees. Trying to get nearer the engine, when we came across something we had not bargained for. To our absolute horror, we became aware that hanging from one of the trees was a parachute, and hanging from this parachute, swinging gently in the breeze, was the body of a German airman. To compound our horror, his grey-green uniform was stained with his blood – turning it into a wine-coloured hue. He must have tried to bail out too late, so his parachute failed to open, and he fell into the tree with such force it decapitated him. We stood speechless, frozen to the spot, and when we backed away another shock awaited us. So intent had we been on the engine, we had not looked around the surrounding area, for we would have found his head which lay several feet away. Somebody had covered it over with sand but the eye-sockets stared back at us. Alongside this spectacle was the charred body of another crew member, roughly covered by a blanket. He must have been blown clear of the explosion. At this point, frozen with horror and nausea, we were aware of the Home Guard and the police who were heading our way and shouting at us at the tops of their voices. That whole episode must have only taken a couple of minutes but at the time it seemed like hours. We were galvanised into life and ran back the way we had come through the allotments to Ponsenby Road, and home. Our pursuers knowledge of the area and their running speed over rough ground could not match ours, so thankfully we lost them. Returning to our home was another trial. Gordon threw up in the garden, and I had a hiding from my mother for getting myself dirty and for being late for school. I can remember that like yesterday.

If you lived in a terraced house – a row of terraces – like my auntie's was, and you were unfortunate enough to have a lamp post outside, it could be a boon in the blackout, because all the lighting was so dim, but in the summer it wasn't such a good thing – they used to put two small angle irons into the pavement at the bottom of the lamp-post, the width of a dustbin – a galvanised dustbin. The irons came up through the handles of a dustbin. Two holes would be in the top and a rod would go through, which used to line up with going under the lid of the dustbin. These were 'Pig Bins'. Everyone, by law, had to put any waste food in them. There wasn't much, but even potato peelings, scrapings of carrots, meat, bones… anything like that. Anything edible that had gone off had to be put in there. Well, you can imagine what it was like in summer! Infested with flies and maggots – the stench would be appalling. You couldn't have it shifted because nobody else wanted them outside their own homes. We used to feed it to our pigs in the war. It all used to be boiled down and fed to the pigs and, yes, we still survived.

Anthony Kingdom

Portrait by Roger Kingdom

Arthur Rugg, born 1938, lived in Embankment Road, Plymouth:

Interviewer: Can you tell me your earliest memory?

I can remember that we were evacuated part way through the war to a farm, I don't remember how old I was but I was very tiny. I remember chasing this duck that had grabbed a big hairy caterpillar I had found. I couldn't get it back, and I was most upset.

Interviewer: Can you tell me what your parents were like?

Well, they were lovely – my father was a Post Office engineer and my mum was a housewife. They never had a lot of money and I was an only child, by force of circumstance rather than choice, and they always gave me everything they could possibly manage. We never had a lot of things, and when you're young, if that's your life, that's what you accept. When I went to Grammar school with all the trips abroad, I never went on those, because my parents couldn't afford it – but it was never a big deal or a big loss.

Interviewer: Do you remember extended family gatherings?

Oh yes, all the time. We still do meet up regularly. My grand-father was offered three houses for all the family, which he didn't take because they were too expensive – they were £500 each on Embankment Road!

Interviewer: What did you do for fun when you were a child?

Well we played in the street because you were able to in those days, and in the back lanes with all the families that were local. There were all the children and we all had our gangs, our Embankment Road Gang and there was Cromwell Road Gang and we used to have little, you know, parleys! Not nasty ones – it was all great fun. Can you imagine children playing on Embankment Road pavements now? We had an amazing experience once. We were playing Cowboys and Indians, and on our side of the road it was raining – and the other side of the road it wasn't! Rain's got to stop somewhere! We thought it was great, we were running backwards and forwards... Embankment Road is not a long way from Tothill Park playing fields and in the back of our street you'd go through what we called the 'hole-in-the-wall' – in that terrace of houses there is an actual corridor. We used to go in through that, and down the hill into Tothill Park and we used to all go off quite happily early in the morning taking sandwiches and things, play down in the park all day, and then come home. Nobody was worried; it was absolutely perfect.

In my grandmother's part of Embankment Road, she had a huge farmhouse table and the family used to all get together and play cards and talk, like they do, and we children would sit on the stairs, or hide under the table, and listen to all the gossip – hearing things that we weren't meant to hear! I can remember we would be there, with cocoa, and Mum would say, 'Come on! It's time you children were in bed!' and we'd say, 'We can't drink our drinks they're too *hot*!' but they would have a skin on them because they were ice-cold!

Interviewer: Do you have any particular memories of the Blitz?

We were evacuated to some farm down in Cornwall. We were on the train and we were coming across the Brunel Bridge when an air-raid started. The sirens went and they stopped the train to put out the coals to prevent any sparks coming out of the chimney. We spent the air-raid on the bridge, with all the searchlights going up and bombs coming down. I remember that very clearly, and I remember seeing a pilot – a plane crashed over Mount Batten and all us children watched his parachute come down.

We had an air-raid shelter in the front of the garden, which we must have used a lot. I can remember there was a butchers shop just across from us, which is not there now. The incendiary bombs came down on it and the butcher rushed over, and all the men in the area were running into our house and passing buckets full of water down the passage, to go and put the fire out across the road. I can remember that. I can remember when a bomb went down the back of our house and took off the whole tenement section and didn't explode – which was very lucky!

Interviewer: Did you have to move out?

No. That was quite interesting because we had a sort of windy staircase that went up, and there was a tarpaulin hung over the gap and you could move the tarpaulin and actually look down into the court-yard. The thing was, I used to sleep walk extremely badly and my parents were terrified I was going to fall out of there. With all the rubble and everything you couldn't go out the back door, it had taken off the toilet – the indoor toilet – the outdoor one was all right, and 77, Embankment Road is about four houses along before another road goes in. To go to the toilet we had to come out of the front, walk all the way around and go in the back door – just so you could use the outside loo!

Interviewer: Did your father build the shelter in the front garden?

I don't know. I think so, it was just a corrugated roof. I think it was an Anderson shelter they had. It was quite interesting because I was a teacher, and just before I retired it became history – we taught the Second World War I suddenly realised I didn't have to look at books, that I could tell the children a lot! I could never understand why I like gardening and flowers, but cannot stand the big purple Flag Irises – the big fleshy ones. I look at them and it prickles the back of my neck... When I was teaching the children about what went on during the war, we went off to a house near my school – I taught at Compton Primary School – to see the inside of an air-raid shelter. The children asked me, 'What was it like (in there), Sir, when you were in the war?' And on top of the air-raid shelter...were Flag Irises! I have not got a single memory of our shelter, and obviously we must have used it a lot, but I have completely blocked that out. It never clicked, until I was in my 50s and doing this for the children, that that must be why this happens to me!

Arthur Rugg

Portrait by Fotonow

Audrey Gladys Uglow, born 8th November 1920, in Stoke, Plymouth:

I think the worst part of the war years was probably going out into an air-raid shelter. There was an air-raid shelter in the garden at Keppel Terrace. My father was in Gibraltar with the Dockyard, so it was just my mother and myself, and we would go out into this air-raid shelter and – you can check this – there were bombs in Haddington Road which was just behind us, and there was one on the corner of Keppel Terrace, because we felt all this rubble coming over on top of this air-raid shelter. It wasn't too difficult to get out – eventually we got out. The worst part I remember of the war years was going into the city to work, I think it was probably 1942, March/April '42, and that was the dust and the smell, the debris and noise of picking up bodies. We used to fill Thermos flasks to get through the night. You just hoped, when you came up out of the shelter, that there was going to be gas or electricity to make a drink, and wash off the dust. Sometimes you'd turn the water tap and nothing would come out, sometimes there wasn't any gas, and electricity might be all you had.

War-time was terrible. The air-raids were awful, the dust, the smells and I think that we all felt that we didn't know if we were going to be alive tomorrow, so we'd just got to get on, do the job, and make the best of it. With my job and the Navy here, there used to be parties at Mount Wise, and at Drake, and we used to go to them all. There was a dance at the Moorland Links Hotel one Saturday night that we went to, and somebody had booked the bandleader Frankie Fuge because the Naval Officers used to enjoy that... The thing was getting enough to wear, because we had to have coupons for clothes. You just looked in the wardrobe, saw what was there, and thought, 'How can I rip this up to make a top for *this* or a skirt for *that*?' For my wedding, friends contributed coupons to buy material, and I made my wedding dress. It was just make do and mend for everything, really.

I manned the telephones for the Fire Service and the HQ for that was in a house called *Wentworth* on Dormy Avenue – just off Seymour Road. I used to work there. If there were any air-raids, or big problems, you got sent into the city – you used to take a little mobile van with you and you'd be stuck in that. I think the worst one for me was when they bombed the railway depots at Laira and I was sitting there with everything blazing around me – sitting in my mobile van. I also did night duty – the city owned Pounds House, in Central Park – and I used to have to man the telephones there. So I worked Wentworth for the fire service, and Pounds House for the city. Well you just had to get on with it. You didn't have a choice – there was a war! I think the only thing you hoped was that the people you loved were going to be safe – it's a very important thing. If you got through the nights, through the air-raids, and everybody was fine the next day then food and clothes weren't really the important things. I was up at up Staddon Heights on V.E. day – I can't remember how we got there, but that's where we were, and we got fireworks from somewhere and everyone was singing!

Audrey Uglow

Image: Fotonow

Barrie (John) Tranter, born 28th May, 1935, in Whitkirk, Leeds:

I knew about the war when I was about five because my father joined the Auxiliary Fire Service. You knew things were beginning to start boiling up a bit on the Continent. And then of course when he joined the Army I knew all about Poland being invaded. It didn't make too much sense to a five-year-old, but I knew all about Adolf Hitler. It was quite strange really because there was the 'phony war' and when it started heating up – I believe Leeds got bombed – Mother decided not to take me to Treorchy in Wales, where she was from, but down to my grandma's in St Austell, at Mount Charles. So we stayed there for a couple of weeks and I was playing in the garden, one day, and I suddenly heard this roar above me and I looked up and this huge plane came over. I'm not telling...this is gospel...you could almost touch it! It seemed like it! And there was a cross on the wings and...I always remember... the cockpit, and there were two men in it. I was only six and I remember...waving! And I was so excited, because the bloke in the back waved back! With that, my mother had come racing out of the back door, grabbed me, picked me up, ran back indoors and the next minute there was a horrendous crash. It had dropped one or two bombs about a mile down the road, nearer the sea.

I remember my uncle, my father's brother Norman, he was in the Home Guard and was a sergeant. Granddad had bought this .22 rifle and Uncle Norman was the only bloke in the Home Guard, down at Charlestown, *with* a rifle, so he was made Sergeant! But he was full of it when he came back home! Oh, he was all about these bombs that had been dropped down at...I think it was Holmbush. But it was so vivid, and later I thought, you know, had I read it, maybe? Or made it up, or what have you? And then one day, many years later, I was reading this book about the history of Charlestown and there it was...all about this incident. So I did see the old German navigator or bomber, or whoever he was, and that was me, ans there was my mother getting me away from the bombs of Leeds and taking me right into the thick of it!

I've got a brother and sister. My brother worked with the Marine Biological Association for most of his working life. My sister, she was born in 1947 during the worst winter in living history. We had snow in the streets for four months and she nearly died. She got infected, with a blocked tear duct, and we couldn't get any coal delivered to have heating... She married a guy whose parents used to run a hostel for elderly gentleman with 'big thirsts' down King Street! So that's them. We are all of us now living in Plymouth. We've all come home, to our second home, because we came to Plymouth actually in 1948. My father came out of the Army and got his old job back on the *Barry Dock News* in Wales, and found out that instead of being a mid-table sub-editor or top of the table, he was back down at the bottom. He saw a vacancy for the *Western Morning News* as deputy chief sub-editor, applied for it, and he had the connections with the West Country so it was a question of...well, his parents had lived at Charlestown, near St Austell...so he got the job.

* * *

I had qualified as a journalist and done my 3 years apprenticeship and I was very involved in the Old Plymouth Society, people like Stanley Goodman. My mentor was Crispin Gill who was the deputy editor of the *Morning News* but very much involved in writing about Plymouth's history. He got me involved and interested in the Old Plymouth Society. When he retired Paton Watson became the consultant. There was a story going around that the MOD were going to demolish the Mountbatten Tower – the Artillery Tower – because the cliff face was cracking up. They'd been using it as a water tower. They'd been told it would cost them thirty or thirty-five thousand to restore and prop up the cliff, and what have you. So we were invited to visit it and turned up en masse with our man, JPW – Paton-Watson. We go up to the tower and we have a look at it, and he looked at it and, 'Rubbish!' he said, in his broad Scottish accent. 'This can be done for £5,000!' So, I wrote an article about it – about this 17th century landmark that could be saved after all, and that the original figures given had been totally wrong and exaggerated. And so there we were. Paton Watson said it could be saved and they coughed up – it was done for £5,000 and it is still there! When I've been to meetings with the Stonehouse residents, I've had to point out to planners that it is not the 'Abercrombie Plan' but the 'Paton Watson/ Abercrombie Plan'. Paton Watson and his team did *all* the legwork. Mr Abercrombie used to come down as a consultant. Everybody used to accuse Paton Watson of demolishing things, but he didn't *like* demolishing things! He was a planner, and he cared about that tower.

Barry Tranter

Image: Fotonow

Barry Woon, born in Stenalees, St Austell, Cornwall:

I was born in Cornwall, but as my father was in the Navy, we moved up to Plymouth. I started off at Mount Street School because when we lived at Headland Park, Father got promoted, so we moved to Peverell. I went to Hyde Park School and then I passed the Scholarship and went to Devonport High School. I had a bicycle when I was about seven, I suppose, and I was a bit of a wanderer. I used to cycle around Plymouth, get lost and then ask people how I could get back to Peverell! We used to spend a lot of time in Central Park climbing trees. There were two old reservoirs which were overgrown, and we used to play games like *Tarzan* in there, because they lent themselves to that with all the undergrowth.

When the war started in 1939 I was ten, and I think we were in Bugle, or Stenalees, for the weekend and I remember being down there when they announced we were at war with Germany. Dad must have come home on leave and we were walking up from Bugle Station – up towards Stenalees – and because he was in uniform this old guy got off the pavement and stepped into the road and said to him, 'I will step in the gutter for people like you!' I felt really proud, actually.

Interviewer: Did your house in Peverell take any damage?

The only thing that happened was next door Mr and Mrs Camp's house had some incendiaries gone into the roof and Mum, bless her heart, she was a fire-fighter down there with this big helmet. They give her a bucket and a stirrup pump and of course she ran in there when they shouted, and helped to put this fire out. I think Mr Camp, who was a driller in the Dockyard, got it out himself, this incendiary. A strange thing with incendiary bombs, if you could imagine a big bowl of rice and you lift up the rice and let it run inside the jar, that was just like incendiaries coming down, they used to come down *hundreds* of them at a time. They would release a bomb, the incendiaries would all come out, you could hear them coming down. In Peverell, we had a big front room and there was just the one bedroom where Mum, Dad and my sister, when she was younger, slept. I slept right by the bay window in the front room. One morning, coming up from the Morrison shelter in our courtyard, I went to pull up the wooden venetian blind in the bay window, and there on the floor was a piece of glass almost in the shape of a bomb – it had fallen out, hit the venetian blind and dropped down.

Interviewer: What's your opinion of the new layout of Plymouth compared to the old?

Well, I can't say I don't like it, but the old Plymouth was more a home. People lived there, they lived over the shops and at night, or evenings, the barrow boys would be there with their lanterns; there was a lot more character with the old Plymouth, and as I said people lived there whereas now once the shops are closed – it's dead. I know it's a lot wider and cleaner, but it hasn't got the same character that pre-war Plymouth had.

Barry Woon

Image: Fotonow

Bernadette Windle, born in the Alexandra Nursing Home, Devonport, Plymouth:

I went to school in St. Paul's, in St. Budeaux and later to Holy Redeemer Secondary Modern School. My brother also went there, and my sister went to Notre Dame when it was in Cecil Street or Wyndham Square, just off Cecil Street next to the Cathedral in Plymouth. I remember lots of little streets and little shops. I can remember the Registry Office in Cobourg Street, which we called a blister! It was a Nissen hut and when we were on the bus we would look out of the window and see the weddings coming out; married couples. There was always confetti on the steps, lots of confetti.

We used to walk everywhere. It was no problem walking – you didn't feel any threat. I think children are more vulnerable these days. I learned to swim at Mount Wise, or that is to say I didn't learn to swim, because it was so cold – they used to take us in April and it was *so* cold! They used to pull us in on a rope and I never learned because it was *so* horrible. There were lots of cinemas in Plymouth, there was what we called the Ford *Bug Hutch*, it's now a place selling wood on St. Levans Road but its still called the Palladium, although we used to call it the *Bug Hutch*.

There were Nissen huts all down one side of Royal Parade – where the Civic Centre is now. I can remember *that* being built, and it was our first sky-scraper! It was fabulous! They had the Youth Employment Office in there on the fourth floor, and we went there to look for jobs when we were coming up for leaving school – I left school at fifteen. They'd have men in the lifts in their uniform…there was always somebody there to do things for you. I think it would be a shame to pull that building down now, because with the rest of Plymouth being built-up, it is really your history of tomorrow. I know the Civic Centre, looks a bit untidy – I wish they could tidy it up a bit – but it shouldn't come down, there's already been a lot lost. Mum and Gran always held a candle to Lady Astor, and Mum used to take me to the museum to see her wedding dress – Lady Astor's wedding dress – it was in a glass case. Over the years it disintegrated and so it was replaced with the first suit she wore to Parliament.

The new shops came up after the war, yes. A lot of them were at the top of George Street. Mostly at the top of George Street and in Royal Parade. Jewellers' shops – lots of different ones. Back then shops were more individual. My sister worked in the Co-op and that was the ultimate – to work in the Co-op – because it was a union shop and you got more pay, and you always got a rise every year without having to ask. So it was the ultimate to go work in the Co-op. I didn't want to work in the Co-op, so I worked in a shop called Mundowny's until I got married in 1969. My cousins used to work in Dingles – they would come in on the train from Princetown to work in Dingles! The train fare was probably all of their wages, but the point was – you had to go to work!

It sounds funny now, but Christmas day we always used to go to the cemetery and put flowers on a grave. We always had nice Christmases when we used to go into the 'front room' and Mother would light the fire in there. That was a treat. Every year she used to buy 'Black Magic', 'Turkish Delight' and 'Orange & Lemon Slices'. Oh and nuts, we used to have walnuts and hazelnuts and dates. The family would come around…that in itself was a treat. Of course then you had the milkman, the baker, the veg man, the coal man, everything was out in the street, you know? Of course you saw people more, and mums in those days didn't work – not usually. It was classed as a disgrace if the woman went to work! Different to now, if you're a stay-at-home mum that's classed as a disgrace! My mother was always home at 4 o'clock. We got home from school and she was always there. It would be unheard of, for a mother to not be there.

Gran lived in Beacon Park Road, at the end, and Mum lived in Swilly at the other end of the road. It was really *all* Swilly, but Gran always said she lived in Beacon Park. My Mum walked from there to the Alexander Maternity Home to have my brother. She actually walked there, didn't have a car. Dad saw him when he was six days old, he was born in 1940, and he saw him when he was six days old and didn't see him again until he was six! My dad was on *HMS Courageous* when it was sunk, and he was rescued. He'd seen a lot of action – he was in the Navy for thirty years. He never talked about it much because he used to say, 'If I talk about it, or I think about it, I'll go mad.' So he was always busy, always cutting the grass or making a table or something, he sort of blotted it all out that way, you know, he saw quite a lot.

I think it was quite hard times because communication

was bad. My mother, she heard somebody in the garden telling another lady that the *Courageous* had been hit, and she ran from St. Budeaux Square to Beacon Park – to her mother-in-law – and they were trying to get information on the radio but couldn't hear anything. Gran said, 'Well, I'm going down to the Barracks, see if I can hear anything.' As she walked down to Drake Barracks my dad was walking up! She said he had on a jacket that was too big, and trousers that were too short, but you can imagine – to see her son! I think it was quite hard for them really, but they were very resourceful.

Cigarettes were always advertised, people now say not to advertise cigarettes, but it never made me smoke, so my argument to that would be, 'Well, it never made me smoke, so why should it now?' But it was a big thing to smoke, you know? You were big if you smoked. My dad used to go to the off-licence, of course, every Christmas, and he'd buy six lights, six browns, bottle of port, bottle of sherry…same thing every year, but he always went to an off-licence – he didn't go in the pub. Of course, if a woman went to a pub she was a – what my mother would call – a hussy!

As a child I *was* aware of all the rebuilding that was all going on. We used to listen to the radio a lot, especially Sunday's 'Round the Horn', 'Life with the Lions', and all that – it was sort of a routine to listen to that. They broadcast when they had done up the Guildhall, and at school we had to listen to the broadcast of it being reopened. I've got a feeling Montgomery – Field-Marshal Montgomery – opened it.

Beryl Edmonds, born 1926, Peverell, Plymouth:

Interviewer: What sort of values do you think your parents gave you?

Well, I think they had good family values. I mean my father was teetotal, he didn't drink, and my mother didn't really, so there were Christmases where we'd have, say, a bottle of port in the house, but that was about it – for anyone who visited – but not a lot of drink or anything. I never knew anyone who went out drinking. I never saw my father drinking all the years that I knew him…and I never, ever heard my father swear, or say anything that we shouldn't hear, as children. He just wasn't like that. He had a a secure job and didn't spend money on things he shouldn't spend money on. I mean we were lucky we had a car, and we used to get taken as a crowd on a Sunday out to Mothercombe and park in the lane there, and then just walk down on the beach…and so we just had that, which I think a lot of people in those days didn't have.

Interviewer: Do you remember anything about family gatherings before the war?

Oh yes! I had one older sister, and we used to have big family Christmases and I mean everyone – when it came to making the Christmas puddings – everyone would go to all the different houses and we'd all do the *stirring*. It was a tradition. When it came to making the puddings then all then all the different families would go along and have a stir, and make a wish, and that was all part of the tradition – part of the build-up to Christmas!

With all the rationing we didn't have a lot of food. My mother was quite amazing how she kept us fed, really. I mean how she managed to do it, I don't know! When you look at the meagre rations we had. But we had quite a big garden where we lived, so we had chickens in the garden. When it came to Christmas and well, they couldn't buy anything, they would have to kill one of the chickens, but my sister and I couldn't eat it because we used to go out and talk to them, and play with these chickens! When this appeared on the table, you know: 'Oh no, we can't eat that!' Silly really I suppose, but probably as the war went on, we may have got more used to eating them, but to start off with we couldn't eat them. Even my father couldn't kill them. My grandfather was the one who was always called on to do the dirty deed, as he'd previously been a farmer.

Interviewer: Let's move on then to the ten years after the war.

Well that would be 1945/'46. I got married in 1949 and had my first son just over a year after, and then I had another one fifteen months after that, so I had the two boys. We tried to get a house because there was no building of new houses being built – hardly anything at all. I would wander around and around, and go to all the different estate agents, and finally I went to one that was in Peverell. This was 1950 and he said, 'Well, I have got one here that hasn't sold...' – apparently the husband and wife had split up, and the husband was living up in Oxford, he worked in the car industry, and the wife wouldn't let anyone into the house! It was part vacant so she was in the downstairs flat and the upstairs flat was vacant. The estate agent said, 'I don't know if she will let you in because she hasn't let *anyone* in before to view it!' Apparently he had just put all the details in the cupboard – didn't think it was worth while – but he felt sorry for me, I think because I was pregnant at the time. So, we went down there, and rang the bell. Luckily enough she had an elder son, who was then about twelve I think, and he was in the house on his own, so he let us in. Well, it was in a dreadful state…they'd been nothing done to it for years, no paint or anything…but it had possibilities. When the woman came home of course, it was too late for her to stop us because we'd already been and seen it and we said we'd have it as we couldn't get anywhere else… Everything needed doing to it – it was in a shocking state! We decided to go for it, and that's how we got our first house!

Interviewer: So you were going to buy the house and she was she going to stay downstairs?

Oh yes. You couldn't do anything about that in those days. If there were sitting tenants they had to stay there no matter what, and you couldn't put their rent up or do anything like that…you had to take whatever they paid. So, from owning the house she then became a tenant. In the end they did get back together again – the husband and her – because, I think, he was ill. He came back down and they decided to move out – so we did get the house in the end.

Beryl Edmonds

Image: Fotonow

Beryl Pauline Pippen, born January 1929, Plymouth:

Interviewer: Can you tell me a bit about your parents?

Yes, my father was a Geordie, from Roker, in Sunderland, and my mother was a Plymothian. And my father went to work in the rope mills when he was fourteen, and when he was nineteen he was caught up in the Great War. And my mother was an apprentice shop assistant for a firm called Pophams in Plymouth – she stayed there until she was married.

Interviewer: And what were the rope mills?

The rope mills were…in Sunderland they made binder twine, they made ropes from hemp. Using imported sisal from East Africa.

Interviewer: How did your father meet your mother?

My mother was living in Lincoln Avenue, in Lipson. Her family lived next door to people who became my aunt and uncle and they were called Waddle. Dad was sent down here for embarkation leave and he promised his mother that he'd look in on her brother (who became Uncle George) and his wife. He knocked at their door and…there was no answer. So he went round to the house next door and knocked there and my mother answered the door and he said he was looking for his aunt and uncle. She said, 'They're out shopping – you can come in and wait.' And that was that! Mind you she had to get out of her previous engagement…they didn't meet again for years but they got married in 1924 in Plymouth.

They went up to Sunderland for a while but then the Depression happened and the owner of the the sisal rope works wanted Dad's job for his own son so he gave him the sack! Then they came down here, and then after that my father worked in the local government, until he retired.

Interviewer: Can you describe the markets in Plymouth before the war?

Well, there was a place called Market Avenue, which was next door to the big covered market and there they had stalls of fruit and things. And if you want to know what it looked like go to Tavistock, they've got a similar big market there. We've always thought that Plymouth market was like that – but bit bigger. And the shops outside were a bit like the shops outside and facing onto the road like in Tavistock. There was Pophams, Spooners and there was Dingles. They were the three main big shops. And then you had a series of little shops in Old Town Street one of which was a toy shop, which I used to glue my nose to when I went by. Then there was a big square of gardens outside what is now St Andrew's Church and there was what they called the Guildhall Square…and there were parades and all sorts of things happened there, and there were a variety of bus stops. But Plymouth was so, so *packed*. If the Germans hadn't come and flattened it, I don't know what Plymouth would have done because the roads were even crowded and packed then…even before the war, when there weren't all that many cars. Because the streets, the *main* streets were very narrow. Really, I don't know what they would have done.

Interviewer: Could you give me some memories of Plymouth in the Blitz?

Oh yes, I can remember the awful wail of the siren. It's funny it still gets my tummy going up and down…there's a siren sometimes sounds in the Dockyard now…I hear this, 'Rrr-RRR' and I can feel my stomach doing it involuntarily – ridiculous really. And I remember that my mother and my grandmother – they were great at embroidery and they sat doing embroidery, during the Blitz and they'd stop, with needles poised if there was a particularly loud bang. I've got two beautiful tablecloths, but unfortunately nowadays one doesn't use tablecloths. One, that my grandmother made (during the Great War), and one that my mother made during the Blitz. Tablecloths with a tray-cloth to match. But the worst Blitz…that was the March Blitz, my father had to go into town fire-watching and he was on duty in the Civic Centre, in the City Treasury which was right opposite my grandfather's workplace – a storage for groceries. He worked for a firm called 'Brown, Wilson, Nicholson' and they had a big factory where the student houses are now by St Augustine's church. They had a store the other side of the road from the City Treasury. My dad was working…fire-watching in the City Treasury on that night of the Blitz when most of Plymouth were bombed. We were sheltering of course, and the all-clear went eventually and…my mother must have been in pieces. I mean she must have been terrified, but she never showed it, neither my mother or my grandmother…did anything…you know, didn't dash out or… they sat perfectly calmly and as a result *I* was perfectly calm. I can remember I was trying to do quadratic equations...in the middle of that!

Anyway, morning came and you could see all the smoke... and still Dad didn't come home. About quarter past ten, my mother, who was obviously watching...with it being the corner house you could see up the road into Freedom Park... said, 'Oh! Oh! Dad's coming!' and she looked again at him, 'Oh my goodness! He must be hurt – he's hobbling! Oh goodness!' Anyway, typical British, she didn't go rushing out to bring him in, she waited until he arrived and she said, 'Are you hurt?' He said, 'No, I'm not hurt – but look at my boots!' And the soles of his boots were completely caked up with some hard sort of stuff. What happened was that incendiary bombs had dropped in on the roof of the Brown, Wilson, Nicholson store and set fire to it. The store had horses in there and the ARP people went in to try and get them out because they were *frantic*. They managed to get *some* out and... they had to let them go...and they just galloped...apparently one jumped into Sutton Pool, in its flight. But there was some horses they couldn't get to, so my dad ran up to the Police Post which was just up the way a bit and asked for a revolver. The policeman said, 'I can't give you the revolver. What is it for?' So Dad explained. During that time, the incendiaries had burnt *all* the sugar in the store and the sugar was running down the road – like a river and Dad was walking in it! It was a very cold March day and so the sugar solidified on his boots! There was no transport, obviously, so he then had to walk all the way home hobbling on these boots!

There was a bomb that fell sort at the *far* end of Salcombe Road, but the little group of houses from Freedom Park down towards Alexandra Road – they didn't have any bombs. All the destruction was done afterwards when they knocked down the factory to make the filling station, and they've knocked that down now to put the student flats up. No we didn't have any bombs, fortunately, down our road but plenty of damage elsewhere. I remember going into school after the Blitz and…we were walking…always had to walk of course, we had no car…went to school and…I noticed that the girl I was sitting next to didn't turn up. We had assembly, and the headmistress, one of the Miss Stranges, read a roll-call of the girls that had been killed. And the little girl sitting next to me had been killed in the Blitz with her mother. But there were no counsellors or social workers coming to visit and give us comfort – we just had to get on with it. We said a little prayer for them and prayed for the families.

Interviewer: And what was it like going through the city?

Oh it was just piles of rubble. I mean we couldn't get into the city, there were no buses running. My father walked into work every day, the City Treasury wasn't bombed… they stepped over piles of glass and swept the place clean and got on with it. If there were fires or what ever it was, you just got on with it…it was a clerical job so, I mean he just hoped for the best. But what I didn't know, and only learnt years after, was that Plymouth people used to go out to sleep on the moors. My grandfather had a shop in Plympton St. Maurice, and it was right behind the keep of the old St. Maurice Castle, with the house at the back.

So we used to go up, as a family, and sleep there some-times. But we found it – going back and forth, back and forth – too much of a job. So after about…it was three or four months I think…we gave it up, and decided we'd stay put as it was difficult for Dad to get to work. He'd have to leave at crack of dawn to get in to Plymouth to his job…nobody gave you any concessions. These days it would be different, but if you had a job you jolly well were expected to get there. They were stoical!

My mother decided, bless her heart, that we'd take in a crippled aunt of mine, Aunt Maud, who had lost her parents so she was given my bedroom to sleep in so I slept on a camp-bed at the foot of my parent's bed. We were all upstairs in this one room. She'd brought her dog with her and by this time *I* had got a dog, a rescued dog from a bombed-out house. So there were two dogs, my mother, my father, myself and Aunt Maud in a one-room, top-floor flat. And we stayed like that for months until Aunty Maud could get into a nursing home. I think my mother was a saint!

The nearest I ever came to any danger was in 1942… long after the Blitz…when my cousin who in the Navy, married his fiancée who was in the WRNS and they came to spend their honeymoon at Newton Ferrers and he asked if I would like to spend the day with them. See, I didn't *know* my cousins very well and here was this great big tall chap…in the Navy and his wife…I was thrilled to bits… 'Yes, I'll come up!' so I went out…we went up to Noss Mayo and we had a walk through and round to Stoke Beach. It was November and quite chilly. Anyway we had a nice walk and got down onto the beach and Joan and I – his wife was called Joan – we were sort of messing about and looking at stones and looking for shells, and all of a sudden we heard an aeroplane and suddenly my cousin was shouting, 'Hell! Get back, back! Back under the cliff!' and so we were running back to the cliff and managed to get there, and suddenly the aircraft appeared and then, 'Buh-buh, buh-buh, buh-buh…' they were *machine-gunning* – bullets everywhere… That was a rogue plane…he must have seen us – these little figures, and thought, 'I'll have a go down there…' That was the nearest I ever came to coming to grief.

I do remember towards the end when the air-raids had became a bit spasmodic – the last air-raid we ever had was about June, 1944 – and we'd been up on the Hoe and the Sound was absolutely chock-full of ships, hundreds of them, they were *packed* in. You could look over to Mount Edgcumbe and you could see all the American army lorries, all camouflaged, and I remember Dad saying, 'My gosh! If the Germans come over now, they'd make a killing!' Anyway, next morning they were *all* gone. The *following* morning we had our last air-raid. It was dawn and we had a really severe air-raid. I can't quite…I know it was light…and one of the German planes had been hit, and the pilot had landed down in Alexandra Road, on his parachute, and of course there were wardens about but they had nowhere to take him – so they brought him to our basement! He was about sixteen-years-old – maybe a bit older… Absolutely petrified. He sat there but I couldn't speak German. They said, 'Well, he'll have to stay here until the Military come and collect him – there was a Prisoner-of-War camp in Yelverton – I don't know when that started... But anyway, this young thing was absolutely filthy, grease all down his face and there was Mum turning up…offering him cocoa. And my father… no it wasn't my father, it was someone…one of the other wardens had a smattering of German from the previous war and he said something to this bloke like, 'It's okay', or whatever…anyway we gave him this cocoa which he gulped down and then we went upstairs…Well I think the womenfolk – that was my mum, gran and myself – went upstairs, and the others stayed down there with him until a Jeep came along and…took him away.

Beryl Pippen

Image: Fotonow

Betty (Ida) Buzza, born 10ᵗʰ March 1932, Woc Road, Swilly, Plymouth:

We had a radio at home, one of the big ones, you know? My brother, he was in the Home Guard. They wouldn't send him to War because there weren't any other men in the family, you see? They always left one man in the family – especially when you had been bombed, and that, and so they made him a Home Guard. Well one night there was this terrible raid and my mother had a good friend of hers who lived three doors away, and she thought she must have been bombed out, because the blast was *so* bad. She said, 'I am just nipping over – only three doors away.' But it was so bad that she got blown right across the road! Yes! She got blown – and we thought the worst had happened, because she didn't come back for quite a while. So one of my brothers went to find her and she was slumped on the ground. She never quite made it to the house, you know? But her friend was all right – and her family. The husband had gone to war and, you see, it was just all these women, on their own, having to do everything.

After our house had been bombed, because down stairs was all right they said my eldest brother could live there and look after it, because there weren't any men around to do anything at that time – they were all in the Army, and that. So they said he could stay there but that we had to go somewhere else, and they always tried to send you to stay with relatives. Well, seeing as I had one sister that was married – her husband's family lived in Gateshead – we all went to Gateshead to live. Except this one brother.

So we lived up there for about four years and while I was there, every time the sirens sounded, I used to scream and scream, you know? So Welfare put me in this convalescence home in a place called Silloth, just on the outskirts of Scotland. Yes…so I was there, and my mother used to come weekends to see me. I was only about six or seven.

We were living in a small house in Plymouth when the Blitz began. There were three of us girls in one bed, but they had me sleeping down the bottom because I was the smallest and all I had was people's feet in my face *all* the time. So that's how we slept until, as I say, we moved. But when we were in Gateshead, it was also very tight, some people had to sleep downstairs, you know? We had a shelter outside our back door was partially underground, but there was a big bit of it above ground, and we just had a cloth across the door, and honestly, when the bombing was on it was shaking and blowing and horrible, you know? You couldn't get to sleep in there. A couple of my brothers slept – they'd sleep anywhere – but I could never sleep there, you know? The noise was terrible because the bombers were always trying to get the Dockyard. Always trying to bomb that. They used to cross the Dockyard on their way back home and if they had any bombs left they just dropped them anywhere. I heard this on the news one day – if they had any bombs left they would try and drop them on the Dockyard but instead of that they got Plymouth most of the time, so it was pretty bad.

You used to hear the news on the radio and you thought, 'Well, everybody is getting it like us', and 'What a horrible world it is', and 'What horrible people the Germans are'. It was funny because when I was about fourteen or fifteen I was at this concert party and two Germans were doing the lights for us, and they were really lovely guys, they really were. They hadn't wanted to go back to Germany after the war. One went to Scotland – to a farm and he *loved* it there because he did write to us afterwards and said, 'I am never going back to Germany any more!' There were German camps in Central Park at the time, and I always had to walk on the other side of the street – I was too scared to walk along where the Germans were! I was terrified because it only had a fence there, that they could have jumped over – I just wouldn't walk by there.

Betty, aged 8, in 1940,
with older sister Emily, and niece Barbara.

Betty, age 21

1953

Betty Buzza

Image: Fotonow

Colin Baser, born 5th September 1932, Fleet Street, Keyham, Plymouth:

I was in in Infant school and the headmaster – I still remember his name – Freddy Granville, took us all out into the playground and told us that the war had been declared and that we were at war with Germany. It doesn't make a lot of impact on you as a child but I think he told us that there would be changes and that we were virtually going into the unknown. That was my earliest recollection of the war.

There was always a family gathering. I had a brother, who was three years younger than me, and a sister, Maureen, who was six years younger than me. We lived in a terraced house – a block of eight houses called Donegal Terrace – which is now called Molesworth Road, in Stoke. It's at the top of Ford Hill. There were always family there. We moved there, I think, when I was five. My grandmother and grandfather were renting the house and they lived downstairs. My mother, father and us three kids we lived in the two floors above. It was a large house, it had a basement, two floors and an attic. My recollection of family gatherings – they always seemed to play cards on a Sunday night! There was no drink involved or anything, they just sat round chatting, they'd play cards with neighbours and aunties and uncles.

I remember the bombings in the night, and me and some of my friends, we used to wander the streets picking up bits of shrapnel from bombs, and that. One of my earliest memories of the war – and it still lives with me for some reason – when a house is hit by a bomb, it explodes outwards and it releases a peculiar odour. It's sort of like its life has gone, you know? It's a smell that I've never forgotten. In fact I did recollect it when I was working away somewhere, and they were demolishing some old buildings and I thought, 'that's the *smell*!' The smell of a building being ripped apart. We used to wander; we used to go down the bomb-sites. I mean, the trouble when you are very young – you don't know any different. You don't know that this is not a normal life. Like I say, sometimes we went to school. There were times when we didn't go to school, but we had fields behind us where we used to play. We had swings, and rope on trees, and things like that. The war – I'm not saying it was a game – but I think it had more impact on the adults – like my mother.

The first school I went to was called Somerset Place Primary, which is virtually across the road from the houses, just off Tavistock Road, Somerset Place Primary... I stayed there and passed the 11-plus – Scholarship they called it – and then I went to Devonport High School.

One thing I do remember about the Blitz – before I was evacuated to Penzance – there was a milk-lady called Olwyn. She was a bit racy, a bit flash. She'd let us sit on her electric motor cart and we'd help her with her delivering. At that time Fore Street in Devonport had been badly damaged and they were building a camp of Nissen huts at the bottom of Fore Street, for the Americans. Olwyn used to give us messages to push through the fence for these 'Yanks' as she called them. And she'd meet up with one or two of them – we were sort of go-between, messenger boys for them! It was always worth it. You might get a bar of chocolate…which nobody else got.

I remember when the Americans entered the war, in 1941, and they started getting involved, and ships were coming over. Because Father worked in the Dockyard a lot of his time was spent on American ships, so our food rations were somewhat supplemented! We'd get tins of butter, and tins of powdered eggs and chocolate – which a lot of people couldn't get – and corned beef and spam, and things like that. He didn't bring home a lot, but it certainly helped. We had a bit more. I've had a think about this, and I don't remember *any* time where I was under-fed or ill-fed. The thing is, when you're young you just accept the situation for what it is. I mean, I know that we used to have sugar sandwiches sometimes. Just bread and sugar… We ate in a very frugal way but it was probably better for us than the way it is at the moment…

Interviewer: What kind of values did your parents instill in you?

Well my mother was…I'm sure lots of boys and girls would say this…my mother was absolutely wonderful. She was like everybody's auntie, you know? She used to give hand-outs to all these cousins, and nephews and nieces…my mother was very generous and kind hearted, and she was very hard working. She was very patient, she was very stoical. She had lots of things wrong with her but she just seemed to get on with life.

Interviewer: Can you remember being given instructions by the Plymouth authorities?

Where the University is now, leading up to North Hill, there's a street that ran up from there – an extension of Cobourg Street – a small incline, and at the top of that was the old Technical College. After each raid they'd put a notice up that would tell you all the names of the people that had been killed. I went up there with Mother, because she'd be worried if she knew there'd been a bomb that there might be someone listed that she knew. In a way a lot of it was quite sad.

One thing I remember – near us was a place called Penlee and there was a big house there – a massive house – well it seemed big to us kids. After a while it became derelict, and we called it 'The Haunted House' because kids dared to go in there, you know? One Sunday morning we went down there and a German plane had crashed in the big fields in front of the house. I never forget, we were so close to it, and there was wreckage of the plane all over the place and one of the Army or Navy examiners there picked up a boot and shook out ashes. Right by us, right where the plane had come down was a tree. Down the side of the tree – all the way down – was blood. One of the airmen had jumped out and been killed, hit the tree when he came down.

After the war, when the war was ended, I think it was V.E. Day, we had a lot of Italian soldiers interned Prisoners of War in Nissen huts at Central Park. I remember on Sundays they were allowed out, and they walked around. You remember they had big round patches on their backs. They never spoke to us.

Colin Baser

Image: Fotonow

Colin Albert Gibson, born 1932, in Adelaide Street, Stonehouse, Plymouth:

During the war we went down to Adelaide Street, to visit my grandfather. We had moved to Exmouth but he stayed in Plymouth because he worked in the Dockyard – he was a carpenter and we came down there in April 1941 and stayed with him. He had a flat, the downstairs flat in no. 20, and we stayed with him. I slept on the chaise longue in the front room, and I can remember in those days when the war first broke out, everyone was very frightened about the air-raids as they were supposed to damage and decimate the whole of the country. When the first air-raid sirens went everybody would dash down to the air-raid shelter for about half an hour or so, then the all clear would go and you would come out again – it was a false alarm! You got so many of these, that in the end you didn't go down to the air-raid shelter – you got blasé about it. I would go to bed about 7 o'clock, in the chaise longue, and the air-raid siren went about 9 or 10 o'clock and I can remember my father coming in saying the air-raid sirens had gone, and to wake up. So I'd wake up, and he'd say, 'Stay there, wait there', and I can remember lying in the dark, because you weren't allowed to have a light on, and my father's cigarette glowing – the light – then all of a sudden you'd hear, 'Boom, Boom! Boom, Boom!' as the guns went off. 'Oh right! Come on! It's time to go!' and off we would go – running along the side of the house and across the road and down in to the air-raid shelters. Where the retaining wall for the Royal Naval Hospital was – the ground inside was much higher than the road outside, and they used this for building air-raid shelters at road level that went straight through the wall and then turned left – they were always L-shaped because of blasts. If they had them long-ways the blast would go down and kill everybody. This particular night we went there and on the right hand side when you went in the underground shelter, you had benches and two-tier bunks that ran the whole length of one side, the other side just had a wooden seat, and usually the women and the children had the bunks and then whatever men there were about, and perhaps some women as well, sat on the seats. The air-raids really got heavy around about 10 or 11 o'clock. Some of the places shook, and I remember the bomb that hit the house opposite my grandfather's was completely destroyed and people were killed there. Roughly some time during the night someone came in through into the shelter and said, 'Who lives at number 20, Adelaide Street?' and my grandfather said, 'We do!' He said, 'Your house is on fire! Go over and save what you can!' The Germans used to drop the incendiary bombs then. The fires would start, and then they would use the fires as markers to drop bombs. So they went out and tried to save what they could, and at about 5 o'clock the next morning my father came and took me out, and said, 'Look up towards the left!' And there was the city centre – it was absolutely just one big red glow – the *whole* of the sky was red. There had been heavy bombing that night. At about 6 o'clock, although we hadn't had much sleep, we wandered back, the all clear had gone by then, and we got to the house and saw that the incendiaries had dropped through each floor until all of the floors had collapsed – just leaving a shell – and where my chaise longue was, was a huge pile of rubble. My father had put his Royal Marine trousers on that chair, and they was buried there, so he had to borrow a pair of trousers from his father then go into the Royal Marine barracks and get a new pair of trousers, and then he was put on a charge for losing his trousers! We managed to save some furniture – pulled it out on to the pavement – the house on the opposite corner was completely destroyed – and they were searching for people when we arrived… There was a woman who lived in the back section of the house – where the doctors surgery is today – and she hadn't been touched by the bombs and she made us come in and we sat with them and she said, 'The boy needs to go to sleep' so I was put in her bed, and I went to sleep.

It was a scary time, obviously; the ground shook at times with the force of bombs, and that acrid smell… I remember an incendiary bomb actually came through the shelter door, on one occasion, and an Air Raid Warden – they used to sit at the entrance to the doors – he tipped a bucket of sand on top of it!

Interviewer: Did you used to play on the bombsites?

Oh yes, that was favourite for us at my age. Because of the bombsites and all the death and destruction, diphtheria broke out mainly due to kids playing and picking up germs… So there was a mass diphtheria immunisation, and we had to go to school and have a jab – a diphtheria jab. Sometimes when you were at school – so many schools were bombed, and especially in Exmouth – that you had evacuees there as well, and what used to happen was half of you would go in for one class session, and then you'd have to go out to play so the other half could come in for a lesson as there just wasn't enough room or paper and things like that. We had to use the whole of the paper – no margins – we had to use the front and the back of the paper...

We were trained to use a gas mask in the very early days of the war, and you had to put it on first by putting it on to the chin then putting it up over your head, and pulling the straps down, and then they used to come around with a flat piece of card and then the snout part – with the breathing part where you breathed in – they used to put a card over the top and blank it off and then say, 'Breathe.' If you couldn't breathe then it was doing its job. Of course kids being kids, especially boys, you'd sit in the back of the classroom with these things on, and you'd get very hot. So we used to pick up the rubber bits *here*...like that...and if you blew hard the rubber would vibrate and make a raspberry-blowing sound and then the teacher would say, 'Who did that? Who did that?!' And we had to try and keep very quiet, with poker faces!

Interviewer: Would you tell me the story about your mother being given the tin of beef?

Oh yes! That was in the early part of the war at the beginning of 1940. The ships came back from Cherbourg with the troops because we were evacuating France in 1940 when the German's overran everything. These troops came back tired and dishevelled, and were all sat around in the road outside Millbay Docks and we happened to come along, and mother was there, and nearby was a café there and the woman in there was doing teas – it was only a small shop – she was doing what she could to help, she wasn't charging anything, and we were passing these teas out to these exhausted men who were all sat in the road. One of them was so grateful and he had a large tin, when I say large, I mean something like a foot high! A beef tin, corned beef, and he *gave* it to my mother as thanks! When my mother picked it up and took it away she discovered that there was a bayonet hole in it where someone must have been trying to open it and, because of that, she wouldn't touch it. She discarded it.

Interviewer: Do you have memories of post-war Plymouth?

I remember VE Day. I slept in the front room, this is before my uncle, my dad's brother who lived with us, came back from the war, and I can remember it was May '45, sleeping in the front room in Langdon Place. All of a sudden, at about 5 o'clock in the morning, there was a big, bright light...and I thought, 'Light? You can't have a light on!' You know? It was *so* bright, and I didn't realise the war had ended and somebody had put a big flood light up there just for devilment – just because they *could*, you know? To show that there was no possibility of an air-raid, and I opened the curtains, and saw this huge light and I was worried...then we realised that the war was really over and the atmosphere was euphoric! People went mad! They were dancing in the streets, and there were parties in the streets within a few weeks of the war ending. They arranged a children's tea party in the middle of the street! I have got a photograph of that, and we sat there – I don't know where they got the coupons to buy the food – but these cakes came from somewhere, and they were full of it, you know? And there was orange juice and stuff like that to drink!

My uncle finally came home from the war. He was in the Navy, and he had had a horrendous war – three times torpedoed. Yes, he went down on the *Valliant, HMS Valliant* was a battleship that was sunk by Italian frogmen in Alexandra harbour, and he was sent home on 'survivors leave' but the ship that he was sent on, a cargo ship, was torpedoed and sank off Gibraltar. Later in 1943, he was on *HMS Abdiel*, which was a fast mine-layer. When the Germans started pulling back from Italy, some war ships took our soldiers into Taranto harbour at the bottom of Italy, as the Germans had left it. They came down into the bay there but struck a mine, and there was a heavy loss of life as the ship went down quickly – but my uncle was saved! Three times he was put in to the sea, and three times rescued; yet when he died at the age of eighty-eight, he still couldn't swim!

Colin Gibson

Image: Fotonow

David James Bernard Bacon, born 5th April 1936, Devonport, Plymouth:

Interviewer: What is your earliest memory?

The one I probably remember most vividly was one of the few times I saw my dad when I was a kid. He took me on the pier in Devonport, so that would have been when I was about three or four. I remember walking out around the pier that was there, and he won me a 'Popeye' doll. I remember being fascinated, and looking down through the slats at the sea underneath.

My dad ran away from home when he was about fifteen and joined the Navy, and he didn't come out until 1948 or 1949, so my mum was a great influence on me, and similarly my grandmother.

Interviewer: Were you aware of your social status? If so, what was it?

Well it was the slums of Devonport, Pembroke Street. Your status just wasn't a concept then; all I remembered is that we were not as poor as some of the people there. You know – we had bedding!

Interviewer: And where did you live?

I was born in Fore Street, and then during the war I lived in Pembroke Street. 84, Pembroke Street. Then in '52 we moved to Clarence Street flats which is only about fifty yards from there, because by then my brothers had come along, and they were demolishing Pembroke Street – it was a slum clearance area. Then we were put into a council flat, a four-bedroom council flat.

Interviewer: What do you remember about your home and your neighbours' homes?

Well my grandmother lived on the ground floor and she had a second-hand shop which she kept the family with during the depression. Originally we just had the top flat, which was a kitchen and a bedroom – that was it. My bed was in the bedroom with Mum and Dad – when Dad was there. As the family got bigger we then took over a first floor room as well, which I remember quite clearly. Mrs Kempster had the front one and I had the back one.

Interviewer: Did you move to a new area between '45 and '55?

Yes we moved. They were clearing Pembroke Street with that slum clearance scheme and moving people to council flats, or houses. A lot of people went out to Swilly. We moved into a four-bedroom flat in Clarence Street.

Interviewer: What was that like?

Heaven! Absolute heaven! If you think before there was Mum, Dad – when he was there – three boys and a girl all in one room! To have a bathroom...that was luxury!

Interviewer: Did it have central heating?

No, no central heating. I think by modern standards it would be considered a bit spartan, but it was heaven for us.

Delise (Florence) Ashworth, born in York, 1922:

Interviewer: How many of you lived in the house at Windsor Terrace, on the Hoe, when it was bombed?

We owned the house and there were five flats in it, all let. We occupied the ground floor, and part of the first floor. My mother's bedroom was on the first floor, and so was mine… The rest was let.

Interviewer: And can you remember whom it was let to?

Yes. In the basement were a Mr and Mrs Hendy, with her mother, an eighty-year-old lady; we were on the ground floor; there was a furnished room let to an army sergeant and his wife. They were there the night before the Blitz when we were damaged, but they were up at the Citadel on the night of the Blitz so they weren't there. The next floor up were two Sisters of the Chapel, who worked from Welcome Hall at Devonport, and they were called Sisters and wore something like a nun's uniform, and on the top floor was an RAF man and his wife and baby.

Interviewer: Could you tell me about your memories of the Blitz?

In the January, we had a raid that set alight the oil tanks at Turnchapel and that meant we had no gas, and we had no electricity either! The electricity came back in three days, but the gas didn't. We had all gas cookers around the house as Mother let the flats furnished. We also had a gas coke fire – there was nothing electric in the house! So we sent up to my aunt in Yorkshire who was married to a farmer. She was the one that I was very fond of who looked after my grandparents when she was single. So she sent up to Aunty Ena who lived in a village, and said, 'I've got to provide some means of cooking for my tenants!' So Aunt Ena got on her bicycle – because Uncle's petrol was rationed – he could only get petrol to get him to the farm where his parents were living, but he couldn't spare the petrol, so she went on her own cycle to another market village, something like the size of Plympton, and found a man in a shop who luckily hadn't run out of methylated spirit stoves because nobody needed them there, so she ordered five, one for each tenant. It seemed to me that we lived on stew – it was very difficult – but at least we could boil a kettle and it was a means of cooking.

Well you see we had frequent raids, of course we did. We weren't entitled to Anderson shelters, I think it was based on income, but two of our tenants…those in the basement and, I think, the top floor…were entitled to what they called Anderson shelters, the curved ones, and they were put up at the bottom of our garden…but during the winter they let in water and of course they were standing in water that night, so we couldn't go down there. So what we did was we went in the cupboards under the stairs in the basement of the house. The dear old lady was in a cupboard by herself on one chair, we were all in the other, and I held the RAF couple's baby in my arms, as the mother was having hysterics – but I did get the baby to sleep! I was very pleased with myself. Also staying with us was a friend of mine, and she'd got her Army Navy cadet boyfriend with her. So we were all down there. The previous night all the soot had come down every chimney, the front door had been blown off, some of the windows had been blown out and we had an incendiary bomb that fell through the bathroom flat roof onto the wash-basin, onto the floor and set alight to the floor! Well we had this army sergeant with us that night, he wasn't on duty at the Citadel, and we had the Air Force man, and between them, using the buckets of sand we were issued, they smothered and shut off the incendiary and saved the building! I mean, it was damaged and with my father being an architect and knowing so many builders in Plymouth, Mother thought if she sent him a telegram and said that we were badly damaged he could get compassionate leave and come down and see the building and get it repaired. That was before we lost the house completely. He got leave and he travelled down the night of the second Blitz and when he arrived Plymouth was in a terrible state because the whole centre of the city was destroyed practically...and our house had now completely gone. But he didn't know that, and he'd come with his case, and he couldn't get from North Road Station so he had to walk all the way round North Road, because there were delayed action bombs all over the place, you could only walk where it was safe...and I remember, that morning, him arriving at the end of our terrace, and I ran to him because he didn't know we'd lost the house, you see, he thought he was coming to a house that needed repairing and instead it was just a smouldering ruin. We were standing around with the tenants...

Anyway that's going ahead of things, but that was how

it affected me, because, you see, we'd been damaged and mother had worked all day and I was at work. I was working in the Dockyard, and then I heard my friend had lost her home further along the road, so I thought I'd go and sympathise with them, and I'd just got home when the siren went and I'd left my bag in the sitting room – I didn't even pick that up! I hadn't put my watch on during the day, I don't know why not, that was still on the bedside table…so I didn't have my watch or my handbag with me – I had nothing. My mother did have her handbag…so we all went downstairs into the basement, and the first thing we knew was these two Naval cadets from Keyham, with their white hats on, I can see them now… You see, the front door had been blown off, so they just walked right in and called, 'Is anybody there?' and we said, 'Yes! We're down here!' and they said, 'Did you know your house is on fire?' Of course we didn't, did we? Incendiaries had come through the roof, right through the top floor flat, onto the beds of the Sisters of the Chapel who were out at Welcome Hall…of course they were feather beds and so they just went up in smoke. Nothing would have stopped it, nothing. When we heard that we thought, 'Well, we can't stay here, the house is on fire!' so we waited for a lull in the noise and then ran down to the Anderson shelters, but my friend and I went back in the house again, because more noise had started, you see… I can't describe to you the *noise*. There was the whistle of the bombs, there was the crashing and explosions of the bombs, and there was all the breaking glass from the falling buildings... There was a cruiser out in the Sound, *HMS Newcastle* she was called, and she was opening fire up to these planes as they were coming over, and when she opened up fire our walls shook, you know? The noise…it really was terrifying. So Doreen and I went back in the house and they all went down in the shelter… and my mother wondered what on earth had happened to me… We waited for a lull and then we went down and joined them…we all sat in the two Anderson shelters… My mother and I had nothing except what we were stood up in – she was in her slippers – we came out and we were standing outside the house which was burning away and a warden came along and said, 'Go up to the Citadel. You can sleep up there.' So we walked up to the top of Lambhay Hill and we looked back at the city burning and it really was a terrible sight. We got to the Citadel and the Army put us up on the floor on 'biscuits' – what they called biscuits – for the night and we all slept on the floor. The next morning and they brought us some tea but they said they couldn't give us any food, as there was a delayed action bomb in the canteen. They couldn't go in there – so they just gave us some tea. Then we walked back and the house was still smouldering and we were still looking at it when my father arrived. And I started crying when I saw him because he was so tired with the journey, and tired with all that walking, and he didn't realise what he was coming home to…

Interviewer: did you get any compensation for the loss of your house?

Not then, not until after the war, and looking back now I can see that we didn't get the full compensation…my father, being an architect, had drawn up plans of what the house had been like and what we hoped to do to it, and, of course, the War Damage Commission would have rebuilt the house, but Plymouth had this *Plan for Plymouth* and the draft of it came through, covering exactly where our house was – showing that we couldn't rebuild – they wouldn't let us rebuild.

Delise points to her burnt-out family home in Windsor Terrace, with Smeaton's Tower and the Naval Memorial in the background.

Delise Ashworth

Image: Fotonow

Derek Alfred Hiscock, born 6th December 1930, in Combe Martin, North Devon:

Before we moved to Plymouth we lived in Ilfracombe, North Devon, it was a semi-detached, rented house. Fairly basic for the time; no electricity, no bathroom. There were basically four rooms and the landlord lived next door. He had retired from the Indian Railways, and was known locally as 'Tiger'. When I was young I liked to hold my own ration card and at that time Cadbury's produced a bar, which they called 'Rush'. It was a 2oz bar in eight squares and I used to ration it out to myself, one square a day with an extra one on the weekend. It was a very dark, bitter chocolate, but it lasted quite well compared with other chocolates. It always seemed to be available, I think, because people didn't like it very much. There was a stage later on, when we came down to Plymouth, where we were able to get hold of blocks of 'Ship's Cocoa', I don't know if you've ever tried it, but it was a solid block that you had to break with a hammer, it really was the bitterest thing but did make very nice cocoa...

My father, a carpenter and joiner, was never called up for the Forces, but with his training experience he became part of the government's 'Direction of Labour' and would go wherever he was sent, working with other craftsmen in the area. A lorry used to pick them up in the morning and take them to Winkleigh where they were building a small satellite aerodrome. That went on for a while, until one day a local police sergeant arrived who we knew quite well as he was a friend of Dad's – I think they were both in the Home Guard together. He came to Mother with a message, 'Tell Alec, when he comes home tonight, to pack a suitcase of clothes and a selection of tools and an Army lorry will pick him up 4 o'clock in the morning and take him to Plymouth.' This was the day after the first big raids in Plymouth and they were gathering in craftsmen to do whatever sort of emergency work was required to houses.

He did that until Exeter had their air-raid and they were transferred, on block there, to do the same thing. Then Plymouth suffered again – the Dockyard and barracks – so they were promptly transferred back from Exeter to Plymouth, and there he stayed. He realised that there was going to be a lot of work potential in Plymouth and he couldn't see a lot happening in North Devon. There was no industry there and he felt work would have been scarce so he managed to get hold of one of the houses his team were repairing, and so we moved to Plymouth, just after D-Day.

I left Ilfracombe Grammar and joined the 'Emergency High School' in Plymouth. When I left there my cer-tificates were sufficient for me to start the professional building route, and I'd chosen the right subjects. It was a medium sized building firm that I went with, they were called 'Spencer's' and they were specialist plasterers. They had two things which they were proud of, they built the Western Morning News offices in town – during the Blitz they were given special attention to save them – and they also did some of the swimming pool on The Hoe. The work that they were doing then was a lot of bomb damage, in-fills, serious bomb damage. What Father had been doing war first aid sort of stuff that could be done quickly, but these were houses that had perhaps been demolished with a bomb. Behind Arlington Road, there were about three pairs of houses, and there'd been a very big bomb and the whole lot collapsed and were burned out, and these were to be rebuilt. We had to clear all the brickwork; we were paid on a daily basis for that. They managed to clean enough bricks – it was done properly with lime-water and they were good bricks – and they had enough, in the end, to rebuild two of the houses. The only thing was, they were continental bricks and they were a different size to what we make in this country! There was a trade, if you like, between this part of the world and the continent. Stuff would go over there and the ship would come back in ballast with bricks, and that's how continental bricks got used in some places here! They always reckoned there were no good bricks worth using in Plymouth!

So that was the sort of thing we were doing, until the company got onto the new estates that had started being built up. The arrangements were that the group Father was with was attached to a major building to be disman-tled – there was no first-aid work required anymore. So he was put on a good scheme that they came up with called the A.M.S. which stood for Apprentice Master Scheme. Basically it was training apprentices by giving them an actual project to do. You'd have three or four trainee apprentices and one craftsman, and they'd work together as a team building a group of houses. They're still there – those houses – in Efford at the bottom of, I think, Pike Road. The first ones on the left as you go up – they were built by apprentices. Father was on that scheme; there were two or three of those going. I don't know where the others are.

At Spencer's the first contract we got was at Whitleigh. I was put out on to the site, in a galvanised iron shed, with a little 'tortoise' stove to do my work out there. They were doing some traditional houses and some 'Cornish unit' houses, which was quite interesting. Next door to us was 'John Laings' who were doing 'easy-form' housing which is non-traditional – not a prefab – its walls are poured into concrete shutters...there are a number that were built before the war, here in Plymouth, for the Great Western Railway – there's some in Peverell if you know where to find them – still as good as the day they were built. So they were there adjacent to us. Unfortunately Spencer's went bankrupt, but at the night-school I was going to, there were chaps from Laing's there, and they had a staff canteen which was right next to us, so I was able to go and eat in their canteen and I got to know them very well. I said, 'Anything going with your lot?' you know, and they said not on the housing, but the power station at Prince Rock was being built by then and they could have done with somebody down there, so I left Spencer's and went down there. Well, it was really civil engineering rather than housing, but that was a good move because the chief quantity surveyor of John Laing's was also the president of the Institute of Quantity Surveyors – whose examinations I was aiming for!

Just after the war a prefab demonstration house went up. I think it was to keep the local populous happy as to what was coming. If you can imagine the Guildhall as it is now, there was a car park beside it then there was almost a look alike block that was the Municipal Office, and then you came out into what I think was Basket Street – now where Royal Parade is. They put this prefab up there and it was open to the public to go and look at. Those curvy American ones were good – they even had fridges!

Later I joined Costain's, who had built the Royal Assurance building. We did the first phase of digging the hole for the Civic Centre. They also did Lloyd's and Pophams – which is now Spooners. Dingles and Woolworth's were the first ones up... My wife will tell you about going to Woolworth's when it first opened and they had all this tinned fruit that you could buy there. It was scarce!

Derek Hiscock

Image: Fotonow

Desmond John Robinson, born 1932, in the Alexandra Nursing Home, Devonport, Plymouth:

Interviewer: What do you remember about your family and school as a child?

Didn't see much of Dad, he was away during the war, he was a Royal Marine and he was away. I didn't really know him until I was about eleven. He spent the war in South Africa. My mother was a busy woman, always doing something. Knitting…I always remember seeing her by the fire knitting. I was amazed once, when we went to a friend's house and she sat down and played their organ, they had an organ and I never knew she could play. She was a keen chapel-goer, church and chapel. She sent us to St Barnabas church, which is gone now, and Sunday School, but she preferred chapel. We used to go down to see my grandmother and grandfather in Luxulyan, a village in Cornwall, and I remember they had a dog, Belle the dog was called, and I remember hugging Belle. We went to live with them during the heavy bombing in Plymouth in 1942 and stayed there until 1945. Mum had to close up the flat and put the furniture in storage.

My school – Sutton High School – had been evacuated to St Austell, so I had to ride about six miles there and back, every day, and I was only eleven. In fact I couldn't even reach the pedals, so they had to put…I don't know…padding of some sort on them, which was embarrassing! One day at school the teacher said, 'Where's your homework?' and I said, 'I'm sorry but I couldn't do it.' We had run out of candles, and there was no paraffin for the lamps and we didn't have electricity.

Interviewer: Can you give me any memories of the wartime in Plymouth?

I remember the whining whistle of the bombs coming down and then the shuddering and us holding each other, I was holding on to my brothers...like stones...I can see that now and the explosions... I remember the noise of guns and bombs and the barrage balloons, they had one in Central Park, and we could see it going up. I remember some of them being on fire.

My brother and I, and there was somebody else with us but I can't remember who, went exploring during the day after the raids, and I remember Plymouth being on fire and seeing all the damaged buildings and rubble everywhere. One memory, which my son often quotes, is of when I saw the pier burning and there were pennies and ball-bearings lying around everywhere from the pin-ball machines that had been blasted – we collected what we could! We shouldn't have gone there because it was dangerous. I remember watching from near the Guildhall demolition squads pulling down buildings and I can see them coming crashing down...

I remember train-loads of French soldiers because we waved to them. They were coming from Millbay Docks to North Road Station and the back of our house over-looked the railway. I also remember seeing a house... and I can see it now...it was in Alma Road, going from Pennycomequick up to Milehouse, and the front of it had been bombed and the whole bedroom and sitting room had been exposed. I remember seeing that.

Interviewer: Did you ever play on bombsites?

No, not on the bomb sites. We used to go, and I can still remember this, to what we used to call 'Tinkies Creek', which was a creek that was where Devonport High School is now, is and it came right up to the road in Millbridge and we used to go and try to find bombs, you know, ones that had gone into the mud. There was a craze for collecting shrapnel, bits of bombs and that. Everyone used to play in the lanes...play football in the lanes. I remember I was home from school once, from Stuart Road School, and I was in bed and I heard a bang – I just remember hearing a bang. It was across the road, and the son of friends of my mother's had found a detonator, and he threw it at the fire and it blew his hand off. Yes, I found out afterwards. These things happened.

Diana Blanche Netting, born in Stanley Street, Devonport, Plymouth:

Interviewer: Can you tell me one of your earliest memories?

Well I think I must have been about three, around 1931, and my dad was in the Navy, and in those days they do two or three years at a time and if they went to China, it would take three years, you know, so I really...I never knew him. But I can remember sitting up in this big bed...I thought it was a big bed, it was probably just an ordinary sized bed...and it was evening, and my mum was going around with the duster, and she was saying she had to get it nice and clean because Daddy was coming home. Well, it didn't mean anything to me − I was just sat up in this bed. The next thing I knew, I was being lifted out of it, evidently Daddy must have come home. I was most annoyed to think that I'd been taken out of her bed... That's the first thing I can remember!

Interviewer: That's a great memory! Can you tell me a bit about your life as a child?

Well, we didn't know my dad because he was away so much and my mum bought us up. We never had a lot, but we were happy. I had a brother, John James, who was four years older than myself, and a sister, Gwendoline Mary, who was ten years older than myself. We only had the bottom floor of a house, I think I had an aunty who lived on the top floor, but we were in a very, very rough district − I don't know if you've ever heard of Pembroke Street, in Devonport? The people wouldn't hurt you or anything like that, but they used to drink, and fight each other, even the policeman went around in twos, it was so rough! But if anybody wanted any money, or charity or anything like that – then they were always the kindest people too. Devonport was our area and we more or less stayed in Devonport; Mount Wise and the swimming pool...I absolutely loved that. And of course we used to have rowing boats, from down Mount Wise, near 'King Billy'. Well, there used to be – probably still are – steps there, and every Saturday or Sunday all the families used to go down there, and there would be these big tough men with rowing boats, and they would get a family in a boat and they would row you right across to Cremyll – over the other side – and we'd have our food and walk up over the top and down and onto a beach, and then in the evening they would be there to bring us all back again. I can always remember the seagulls, going down into these rowing boats on the sea, and we used to think they were lovely. Of course now they're seen as pests, aren't they? I can remember being taught how to swim, my dad and my uncle ended up with their own little rowing boat and I used to run around – I must have been very small – and he put me on the oar coming out of the boat, and I'd grab it and he'd say, 'Swim! Swim!' and then he'd gradually take the oar away and that's how I learnt to swim... I used to love the water.

Interviewer: Can you remember where you were when you heard about the German invasion of Poland?

Yes, let me see... I can remember when France fell. I was up in Fore Street at 11 o'clock on that Sunday morning, when war was declared. I can't really remember much except I was going to school at that time, and because a lot of schools had been destroyed, one group would go in the morning and another group would go in the afternoon. I can remember walking down the street on my way to school and my sister, was coming home from work and she said to me, 'We've had it now! France has fallen!' I can remember that and thinking, 'Oh Lord! We've had it now!' but I was still really too young…I didn't realise the seriousness of it at all.

Interviewer: Where was your sister working?

It was a place up in Marlborough Street, it was called Swiss's, Swiss's printing works, and they used to do all the programmes. There used to be the Alhambra Theatre (Tavistock Street) that used to do all the live shows – they were fantastic at that time… Something like the Palace used to be…and the firm that she worked for did all the programmes and all the posters, and I used to love going in to meet her to go home, and she'd be stamping these programmes with numbers, and I said, 'I'm going to do that when I grow up! I'm gonna do that!' So that's where she worked, but that eventually got bombed and she ended up in munitions – she worked in Ernesettle Munitions. They used to do so long in certain parts, and they used to turn yellow after a while, so they could only do so many weeks at a time. It was something that they were working with – the explosives, or whatever it was.

Donald Frederick Evans, aged 87:

I was born on the 9th March, 1927, at 3 and a half Gibbon Street – I don't know where the half came from! The house our flat was in was in the middle of Plymouth, on the corner of the junction of Gibbon Street and Clarence Street and opposite the Clarence pub – roughly where the car-park for Charles Cross Police Station is now. There were no traffic or cars so we used to play in the streets. My dad, being of militaristic mind, bought lots of little pistols, and things, and we used to lend them to our mates and then run around the streets playing Cowboys and Indians, shooting each other you know, the way kids do, or used to. Just in that little area we were free to roam where we liked. Except once when I was very small – two I think, and Pete, my brother, would have been three, we were picked up in Ebrington Street by the police. They found out where we lived and they brought us home. I don't remember that but at regular intervals I would be told about it. My parents gave us independence, they expected us – and I think this is better than discipline – they *expected* us to behave in a certain way, to behave properly. We were never punished. No, they weren't strict in any way. On one occasion in school – I went to the Grey Coat School – a teacher whacked me on the back of the hand with the edge of the ruler. When I got home my dad saw it and said, 'How did you get that?' I suppose I was about four or five. I told him. The following day he went to the school, hauled the teacher out of the classroom and told him that if he ever laid hands on me again, he'd beat him to a pulp! Dad had been a boxer in the Army. I was never touched again after that.

Plymouth had six hundred or so air-raid alerts but most of them didn't come to anything. Then began occasional air-raids with bombs here and there, so my dad decided we were to have an Anderson air-raid shelter at the bottom of the garden, so we set to digging the hole and we assembled the Anderson two-thirds down into the hole and you then throw the earth you've dug out on to the top in the hope that it might stop something. Pete and I were shovelling soil on top of the Anderson shelter and we heard a droning sort of noise. We looked around and couldn't see anything, and then straight up there was a formation of German aircraft in a beautiful diamond shape. I counted about fifty small crosses, silver crosses with a bigger darker cross in the middle. They kept their course over the Dockyard, over us, out towards the moor, made a turn back in again then flew away out to sea. We had very little anti-aircraft protection at the time. Most of the protection came from *HMS Newcastle*, a cruiser. I realise now that was an aerial reconnaissance – photographic reconnaissance – but I didn't know at the time. We all dived in the shelter until they'd gone!

As bombing became more frequent Dad got us to sleep regularly in the Anderson shelter through the winter. He made a bunk for Pete on one side, and one for me on the other and a little one across the end for my brother Terry who was then four. Mum and Dad slept on the ground, in between, so if a raid came along we didn't have to get up and go there, which Pete and I used to hate, you know, down the garden in the cold etc. One evening there was an alert, but nothing happened, so we came back out of the shelter and were sitting in the living room having a drink of cocoa before going to bed again. Suddenly there was the most almighty bang – the loudest noise I'd ever heard. No sound of any plane or anti-aircraft fire or anything. I went to the front door and found the front door had been blown off the lock! There were two holes in the roof, and the garden filled with dust and debris. This was because one bomber had dropped one bomb at random, probably heading for home. It had dropped behind some houses on the other side of the street and destroyed a little terrace of three houses and killed a family of four called Pomeroy. We went back in, to sort of recover from all this, and Dad turned up about half an hour later, in shock, because somebody had said to him that a bomb had dropped in Chard Road, where we lived, and killed a family of four. He left everything and came home and found us. Nobody would have stopped him I think.

Well there came a night when we had an alert and we were all in the shelter, tucked up in our blankets and we heard some distant anti-aircraft fire. It came closer and we heard that noise German aircraft used to make, a kind of throbbing noise that came from the twin engine… vmm-vmm-vmm-vmm…rather threatening. Then bombs started falling over the Plymouth and Devonport areas. We came to realise this was different. This was something more purposeful, not just a random raid, and it went on heavy, heavy bombing for hours. We all had steel helmets as Plymouth was awash with military gear after Dunkirk, and Dad was in the Home Guard. The Home Guard had to carry a gas mask and helmet wherever they went, and what he did was to go into the Dockyard to work of a night without a helmet, and then he'd come out with one – so we had all these helmets. My younger brother Terry, I remember, had a little French one – a little blue French one. Anyway, every so often during this heavy bombing, Dad would put on his helmet and go outside and look around and see what was happening. On this occasion he came back and he called to Pete and me, 'Come and give me a hand! The house next door's on fire!' The water supply had been cut so there was no water. 'Go and get a washing up bowl each and get some earth from the garden and bring it up to me, upstairs, next door.' The aircraft were overhead, they were dropping parachute flares, little white flares that lit everything up brightly, you know. Searchlights probing round looking for them, flashes from anti-aircraft guns, shell bursts up in the sky. The sound was pretty terrific, bombs bursting – some not very far away from us. There I was with my little washing-up bowl of water and earth, running across the garden to take it up to Dad and suddenly I found myself on my hands and knees. I looked behind me and I saw what looked like two poplar trees growing slowly up into the sky. These were bomb bursts and one of them must have blown me off my feet! My memory now is like a vivid picture, I can see it any time I want, it's there – that particular little bit. The incendiary bomb had come in through the roof, through the ceiling, landed on a bed, burned through the bed, landed on the floor and was burning through the floor and would have carried on burning through. We supplied Dad with earth, he was in there throwing it on the bomb and stifling it. Eventually he was able to sort of kill it off. Smoke…orange flames… everywhere, I remember, and Pete and I said, 'Can we come in and look?' 'No!' he said, 'Bugger off!' So we did. Back into the shelter we went, got through the night and the following day we walked up through the garden and it was quite awesome. You could see the whole of Plymouth and Devonport from where we lived, all burning…the fire reflecting off the clouds. It was sort of apocalyptic, if you like. That's what it felt like to a boy of fourteen.

Anyway, the next day, for some reason, I decided to go to school – I don't know why! My school was Stoke Senior Boys Elementary School in Devonport. There was a sort of skeleton bus service still running in as far as it could run. All the buses incidentally were painted grey. Whether they'd been given grey paint by the Navy, I don't know. Some had windows, some didn't. I found a bus and it went so far towards Devonport but then the driver stopped and the conductor said, 'This is as far as we can get. You'll have to walk.' So everyone got off the bus and started trudging along through wrecked streets, and fire, and smoke and debris and I remember a sort of musical sound – it was hundreds of people walking over broken glass – quite strange. I made my way, tortuously, through the streets. Some streets were closed off with a sign saying 'unexploded bomb', others were flattened anyway, some were burning, with rescue teams digging in them. To get to Fore Street in Devonport, the best way was to walk across the parade ground of the barracks. The barracks were all flat but with a parade ground there was nothing to block you, so a lot of people were cutting across like that. I got into Fore Street and walked down it and the whole street was either flat or burning. All the cinemas, department stores, churches, pubs…everything. I got to the end of it, to Morice Square, the school was in a little street called King Street which led off Morice Square. I went into King Street, which was either burning or flat, from end to end, and I stood by my school looking up at it. It was an old, four or five-storey, Portland stone building. I was looking up at it thinking not so much, 'This is great!' as most boys might, I was thinking about my new ruler and pen I had bought a couple of days before, and that they were up there somewhere in my desk, burning away with everything else. A teacher, Mr. Swords, came along and stood with me for a minute or two and said, 'Well Evans, not much point in you staying here, you go on home and we'll get in touch with you.' He didn't know, and neither did I, that the school records office had also gone up in smoke in Coburg Street, so in effect, I didn't exist as a school-boy anymore, and that was really the end of my formal education – that day! I never went back to school.

Plymouth was filled with American sailors, soldiers, and stationed all round the place were their anti-aircraft guns and things, quite close to us were some of them. The Hamoaze itself was filled with landing craft as time went on. In rows and rows and rows, all the way up to the Lynher. There wasn't much in the way of entertainment obviously, you couldn't go near the beaches because they were mined and barb-wired, so my mates and I used to ride around on our bikes. One day we were up on the moor, out Roborough Down way, and we heard a rumbling sound. We looked to the north and we saw a Lancaster bomber appear, then a couple more Lancaster bombers and two or three more, and more and more. I started counting as this stream of Lancasters flew up over us and out over the channel. I counted ninety-six. It's strange to think that people now go miles just to see one Lancaster! They were heavily laden, you could tell they had bomb loads. This was in the run up to D-Day, so they were going over the channel to bomb the hell out of something. I didn't see it that way then, I felt a sense of relief. My mind went back to my first sighting of German aircraft, fifty-odd of them and here we were with one hundred or so Lancaster bombers of our own, and it was satisfying. It's not supposed to be, nowadays, but there we are – that's the way we felt.

Plymouth city centre itself, you weren't allowed in straight away it was so dangerous. By the time I was able to get in there, that was in as bad a state as Devonport – worse really. They were clearing some of the streets, through the rubble, so that cars could get in. That would be George Street, Cornwall Street, Bedford Street, Drake Circus as it was then. The only building left standing was the Prudential Insurance building, this was a tall red brick building. It was rather attractive, but in their enthusiasm for change, they knocked it down. They could have left it – but they didn't. I can remember the cinemas were all gone, the Gaumont, the Odeon you know. Wandering into

Plymouth and looking around I remember seeing a tall dwelling, several stories high, which had been sheared right down the side and there was a conventional picture of rooms exposed to the fresh air with beds hanging on the edge of the floor you know...pictures still on the wall, that kind of thing. I can remember seeing that. The Barbican suffered although not the old, old bits. Apparently there was a school of thought to tear all that down and start again! All those Elizabethan houses – get rid of them! There was a 'Save the Barbican' group as well, and they carried the day.

Donald Evans

Image: Fotonow

Edward William Luscombe, aged 87, born in the Stonehouse Maternity Ward, Plymouth:

One thing I remember is that my school, Sutton School, was on a slightly rising slope. We had a basement with windows on the south-facing side but the back was against the ground, as it were, so they converted that into a shelter for the school. All the south-facing windows were built up with sandbags, and the older boys – their job was to fill the sandbags, which they did. That meant us younger ones didn't go to school for a fortnight until they'd done all that! All these bags were put up against the windows so that was the air-raid shelter for the school. Eventually they built an underground shelter in the car park, well it wasn't a car park…a playground, and so I am pretty sure that there are many all around the city. They'd dig a pit and make a concrete sort of tunnel-like thing and cover it over, of course. Again, it was for protection. But you can't do much about direct hits wherever you are. Anyway, that was in the very first days of the war. Of course, not much happened at the beginning of the war.

Interviewer: Would you always go to your shelter at home when the siren went?

I think so, the sirens went two or three times a week. I remember, on one occasion, the siren had hardly gone and we heard this terrible, loud whistling noise of bombs coming down – they went over our house and crashed on the railway estate, the road above Church Hill Road, killing people. Those bombs were pretty near us, but on the whole, in Wesley Avenue, we didn't have any direct bombs although there was one up at the top at Oxford Avenue. I remember my father, and the man below us, were outside and they shouldn't have been, and they heard this whistling so they scrambled into the shelter, but before they could really get in there was this huge… mind you, we were a quarter of a mile away…so they weren't damaged in any way, but that was the closest…

In the shelter we might try to do homework, might try to do a bit of reading. The man downstairs had put a cable from the house into the shelter and so we had a light, and we also had a little bowl fire because it wasn't very warm. The entrance was sort of covered with a heavy curtain. But we had a wall at the other side so that offered some sort of protection. Like a blast wall. It just happened to be there. Some of the people made their air-raid shelters really very comfortable.

Then of course there was Hyde Park School, which had incendiaries dropped on it and the top of the school was burnt off! My sister's classrooms were there – I had left by then – and all her stuff was burnt. The day after one air-raid, I went down to my school, the Emergency High School for Boys, which was in Regent Street. It was on a Friday I think – and opposite the school there was a tenement block and it was just a smouldering ruin, but our school was saved because there had been senior boys, and the caretaker, on the roof pushing the incendiaries off, and that building is still there to this day.

In January '41 we had a very serious raid on Plymouth when bombs fell on the oil tanks at Turnchapel and it caused a huge fire with masses of black smoke all over the city. We were concerned about that because it meant the next night the area would still be lit up and would alert the bombers again. But I don't think they came back. But that night the serious damage was that the electricity was cut off, and the gas. We had no electricity and no gas. The electricity came back after five days but the gas took about six weeks. Even at school – the Bunsen burners – we couldn't use them because we had no gas, so they bought spirit burners to help us with our experiments.

Interviewer: So life carried on as normal? You still went to school?

Yes, we went to school and of course we had a shelter at the school. By then they had stuck one in the playground and we had to get in there a few times. We used to walk to school, and walk home, and I can remember walking home once and we could hear aircraft and we actually walked right into Portland Square underground shelter. We just happened to be walking by that way on the way home.

Interviewer: Do you remember troops coming into Plymouth?

Yes, we were all very concerned because France had fallen, people were talking about it and there was a sense of trepidation, 'Oh dear, what's going to happen next?' I think obviously more so for adults. Don't forget young-sters tend to not be so worried, but it does rub off from adults. We went up on to the Hoe and saw what were, possibly, Belgian troops marching up. You know they had come off a ship, or something, all the main evacuation was obviously over in the Thames estuary, but quite a lot troops ended up at this end of France and came across to us. So I do remember seeing such things, yes.

Interviewer: What about the rebuilding of Plymouth?

Well, of course, in 1943 out came the Abercrombie 'Plan for Plymouth', which was very exciting! There was an exhibition and pictures and maps, and all this sort of things, as to how it was going to be after the war. The book that came out was a really wonderful thing. It cost 10 and 6 – a lot of money in those days!

I am glad that I was old enough to remember the original Plymouth and can recall in my head things like travelling on the tram, and going past the shops and everything. What we used to do as children is that the trams were open-top and the very first thing we would do when we got on the tram was we'd run upstairs and straight to the front. Then we would kneel on the seat and look out to see where we were going. We would *always* do that if we possibly could, and so my retained memories are going from the Theatre Royal, Princess Square, Whistles Street, Basket Street, Old Town Street, past the Spooners, up the hill via Old Town Street and then past the reservoir, up North Hill, onto Mutley Plain and from Mutley Plain around into Peverell where we got off. So I do remember all that, and it is nice to be able to. It was an exciting time and to think Plymouth was going to be re-built, but there were a lot of disappointments about what happened in the end. The pattern of Plymouth before the war was lost.

Edward Wilkinson, Plymouth:

I was born early in the war, 25th Nov 1940 in the Alexandra Nursing Home at Stoke – I'm not sure if it's still there – but I was born in the middle of an air-raid, I'm told by my late mother. Apparently at the time of my birth the *Luftwaffe* had hit the gasometers at Prince Rock. Consequently the city was covered in smoke for three days, and the electricity supply to the nursing home was not working, so I think an oil lamp was bought into play at the right time! My father was away in the RAF, so I didn't really see much of him until the end of the war. I can see him clearly now in his uniform, he occasionally bought home model airplanes that he'd made for me – that was rather special. My mother was constantly caring for me – I was the first – I had two brothers who were born after the war so I was the only child at that time and so she was my complete support mechanism, but even at that very early age I detected in her an anxiety, as we were subjected to quite a lot of air-raids over Plymouth, particularly in the area where we lived.

I think my earliest memory would be receiving the training protocol from my mother, which necessitated being put into what was called a siren suit, which was like the forerunner of the tracksuit. It zipped up so you could take the child out quickly to the air-raid shelter. It's interesting – I heard the word being used about two months ago on some television programme, it was specifically designed for children in the air-raid shelter. The idea was rather than mess around with all the bits and pieces and clothing and nappies, you put the child to bed in that suit and you could have the zip undone if it was too hot in the cot, but if the 'visitors' were over head, you could zip it up, grab the child and go. It might have been the original *onesie* but I'm not sure!

We lived in a flat in Mutley, which was close to the railway line, so we were probably 200 yards from the main Paddington/Penzance line and consequently a target. There have been maps produced with black dots on, showing where the concentration of bombs were dropped, and as far as I can see, they were obviously concentrating on the Dockyard area, because of the Admiralty and Devonport support systems, but also the railway line was a main target, so we had quite a lot of activity there, a lot of false alarms but also actual raids. That was a part of the problem, because when the siren went off you didn't know whether you were in the firing line or if it was a false alarm. It all played on the nerve-ends. I think, if I'm right on reading the history, there were thirty-nine 'live' raids in that section during that period and a lot of false alarms.

Interviewer: Was it permissible for you to play on the bomb-sites?

Not really no, no. There were notices up, 'Dangerous building, do not approach', but we just climbed under the red and white tape and climbed on the structures – you'd be horrified if you thought your grandchildren were doing it but as far as your mother was concerned, she didn't know – she was back at home – it was 'out of sight out of mind'. Strangely, and ironically, it was a safe environment in many ways because of a complete lack of traffic so there were never any concerns about road safety. We would improvise, which was probably good for one's development, things you'd make up from bits of old prams, trolleys you'd found on bomb sites, bits of board and string, like a go-kart...without any brakes on it...we'd go speeding down hills at crazy speeds, so you improvised with the bits and pieces you found to entertain yourself, and build dens and what have you, on the bomb sites. It was a fun playground in a way – sad somebody's home had been destroyed but we were kids and it was sort of like a magnet – kids got drawn to it – just to see what they could find and what they could do with what was found.

Interviewer: Did you have any interaction with the American troops?

We had a bus-stop outside the house and I remember, one day, two American sailors standing across the road – it was like one of those Hollywood movies, with the pork pie hat and all that stuff – apparently I went over and said, 'Have you got any gum, chum?' They responded and gave me some gum! Occasionally you would see their amazing vehicles, big wheels I remember, huge tyres. Everything was bigger that came out of the U.S. compared to our vehicles, occasionally you'd see one going through the area.

Interviewer: Did you go into the city centre at all?

I learnt to swim, aged six or seven, and I went to the pool up on the Hoe – Tinside. I remember walking from

Mutley down through Tavistock Road, there was an old pannier market along there somewhere which was almost made up of bits of old Anderson shelters, and that would get very busy. You could get some fresh vegetables there; it was a good place to go. People just made up these stalls from whatever they had, and sold their produce, whether it came from their gardens or allotments...but passing that...which was the highlight of Plymouth shopping in those days as there was nothing else – you'd come down through the rubble, right across all the bomb sites and on the way up to the Hoe there was one ice-cream shop, standing in isolation. I think the company was called 'Williams'. Everything around it was flattened, but somehow they'd kept going and on the rare occasion you had enough money to buy yourself an ice-cream it was a big event – even as late as the '50s. But the trip to the Hoe, across the bomb sites, down to the pool, I think it was a penny to get into the pool, and a penny for the Brylcreem machine, so you wanted 2p for your journey, 3p if you were lucky because on the way back you'd be very hungry after swimming, and in another solitary shop standing down near where the old Corn Exchange used to be, they sold bread, I think, but they also used to make what were called 'Nelson Squares', it was really like a baked bread and butter pudding...and they were a penny.

Eileen Organ, born in Knighton Road, St Judes, Plymouth:

My Dad was a captain in the Merchant Navy and Mother was lovely. I had sisters and I had a brother, 12 years older than me, who was in the Navy and I married two husbands in the Navy...I enjoyed being a Naval wife. My parents had a lovely house in Knighton Road, down here.

I was born in 1922 and we all grew up together – we were a close-knit family, because in those days people didn't move away like they do now. I went to Salisbury Road School and then I passed the scholarship so from there and I went to Corporation Grammar, and yes, I had a happy childhood. Oh I loved history, it was like stories, I quite liked languages. I was taught French, Latin and German, trigonometry, algebra – I'm rusty now, dear! I didn't like swimming, or hockey when you had to 'bully off'. I liked tennis and there were ropes, and I liked climbing up to the ceiling. Yes, I liked gym. I left school when I was sixteen in 1938.

Mum always kept a good table; on a Friday we always had fish, Mum was not a Catholic, but we always had fish on a Friday. On Sundays we had a roast, and on Mondays we had cold meat and that...but Mum's pasties and her dough cakes and dough buns – Cornish – her pasties were lovely. My first husband was French, so I became fluent after Dunkirk. I met him at a dance in the Guildhall for the Free French, and of course being fluent...well...we got married!

During the Blitz, my husband was at sea on a ship, and

I'd asked my friend to sleep over with me. Well of course my husband's ship came in, so I had to put my friend in the front room and there was a blast and she ended up with the Venetian blinds all around her, oh, she did look funny! Luckily, Jill, my baby daughter, had turned over in her cot...and I had the wardrobe over on me! Fortunately I didn't know I was pregnant with John...

I think the war brought people closer together. Neighbours were nice and you helped each other in those days. Now you don't see your neighbours – you don't, do you? I could go out and leave the doors open then...I wouldn't do that now. People would come in the back and go out the front, or come in the front and go out the back. We were the last house. It was a never ending open door... I mean the insurance man, the refuse man...all used to pop in, have a cup of tea and a biscuit and have a good old yarn, you know?

(Daughter Jill: Mum would be up with Nan, and if my brother and I came home from school we knew the key would be in the oven, so we could get into the dining room! The scullery door and the back door were never locked.)

After the war, for social activities, we'd go to the barracks on a Sunday, go out for a drink with friends on Tuesdays, and on Saturdays go up to The Mayflower Hotel, it's called now. We had a nice life with lots of love and loads of friends.

Elsie Hobbs, née Sprague, living in Laira, Plymouth, aged six when war was declared:

A lot of the families didn't want their children evacuated. They used to say things like, 'We'll all die together', that sort of thing. Many of the children went to relatives outside Plymouth or even further away from Plymouth. It was dangerous to be in the city and a lot of my school friends were killed. I remember coming into the classroom one morning, at Laira Green School, and one child would say, 'Mummy's received a telegram to say Daddy's lost at sea, presumed dead.' Or you'd go in and find an empty seat, and the teacher would say, 'Well, Barbara…' or whatever they were called '…was killed last night in the Blitz.' You didn't have counselling, there was no such thing as counselling. Often we'd been up all night because of the Blitz, bearing in mind the raids used to start anywhere between eight and nine of an evening and go on sometimes until half past five in the morning.

I have always had good hearing and I would be able to hear these planes coming in the distance from the direction of Germany, or France. It was an awful sound getting louder and louder and the first thing that happened would be one plane would come over on its own, I think it was called a 'Pathfinder' but I'm not too sure about that. They would drop flares all around the outskirts of Plymouth so Plymouth was lit up like daylight. Then you'd have the onslaught of planes, after planes, after planes. The first thing that would happen is that they would circle the outside of Plymouth with incendiary bombs and fire bombs that would set Plymouth really on fire. I can remember you had the stench of the fire where the shops were burned out. After that they would go and another wave of planes would come – it was relentless for hour upon hour. You could hear them coming, it really was relentless bombing in the nights of the Blitz. After they dropped the incendiary bombs they would drop their high explosive bombs and then their unexploded bombs and they were feared, those unexploded bombs. All you could see were big craters where the bomb had gone in but not exploded. These bomb disposal men would come with their lorries and detonate them or carry them away. Mainly carry them away and make them safe, and then we'd all cheer on the pavement as the bomb went past us, I can remember the fin on the back of these bombs on the backs of the lorries. My memories of the Blitz are horrific. We'd sit, terrified, absolutely terrified, all night these shelters which were cold, damp and horrible. We shivered, we were fearful, we could hear the bombs coming down and we would all put our heads down and put our arms around each other. Sometimes I used to go in the next-door neighbour's shelter because often my mother wouldn't be able to walk down to the shelter and she would say to me, 'Elsie, you run into the shelter, I will be all right.' She had so much faith in her God that she was going to be all right, and she was. My father was often working on the railway so he wasn't there. He had so many different shifts of work but he was mainly working nights. If you could hear the bomb, it was said, it wasn't really meant for your patch – and that was mainly true.

It was a different way of life all together but we all coped and we all managed – we had Double Summer Time and there was the six months of daylight at midnight. There is something I ought to mention about Laira Green School. When I eventually returned from evacuation in Truro and went back to school, there was one lunch-time when we were walking home for lunch through a road called Beverly Road, in Laira. There were about eight of us girls, all about nine years old, and we'd been taught lots of different lessons about bombing. When you heard a plane coming down low behind, you should run and fall into the gutters, face downwards. We all heard this plane coming and we just dispersed, and ran into the gutters. I can still see the shells now, going up through the road where they machine-gunned. They were really machine-gunning children. We looked up as the plane went over us and we saw this big black swastika on the bottom of the plane, and we could see men in the plane. Another time, one night, my father was actually in the shelter with me and my mother and he said, 'Come outside Elsie, I want you to see something.' I didn't see the German plane shot down but I did see the Germans parachuting down over Mount Gould.

Regarding food, Dad didn't like bacon so he'd give his ration to my aunt, and she would give him cheese in exchange. The next-door neighbour had three children, and my mother was always aggrieved that she would get a pint of milk a day. I was an only child and so my mother was rationed to half a pint every day, apart from Sundays and then she was allowed to have one pint. She scalded all her milk to be able to get a little bit of cream on top.

We didn't have more than one pound of jam, to go on our bread, for the three of us per month, so when the jam was gone…the neighbours did a lot of my mother's shopping, and they would go into a chemist and buy jam, which was baby-food like jelly, bramble jelly but because we grew blackberries, or had blackberries and apple and pear and plums in Britain, our jam was normally plum and apple or raspberry jam. You had substitute sugar, you had substitute coffee. We didn't have tea bags, we had packets of tea, but they were limited per family – that was rationed. Anything that was only grown abroad like coffee and tea and certain fruits were limited. We didn't get many boats with bananas or oranges. There were three different coloured ration books. One was buff for adults – anyone over fourteen. Fourteen was the cut off age, whereas now it's sixteen or even eighteen, but because children left school at fourteen you were considered to be an adult unless you went to Grammar school, then you had to stay on until you were fifteen. So that was an adult ration book from fourteen plus. The baby ration book, up to the age of eighteen months, was a very pale green. The children's ration books were blue, eighteen months to fourteen, so I had a blue ration book. If a banana boat did manage to get through the convoys, only babies under the age of eighteen months were eligible for one. If a boat came through with oranges the children with blue ration books were included with the babies to have one orange. I probably had one orange every nine months to a year. I remember one neighbour had a baby, and so there was one banana in the household, and this lady, called Minnie Aldgate, chopped up the banana in as many little pieces as she could and called all the children in the neighbourhood in. We all tasted the banana, just a little bit of it, because we'd all forgotten the taste of them – so you shared. You shared everything; you shared your life with your neighbour.

Elsie aged 3 or 4 with her cousin Arthur Sprague
in front of Plymouth Pier on West Hoe, before it was bombed.

Plymouth was a small city in comparison to what it is now. I can remember when the first housing estates, council housing estates, were built. Plymouth extended then past Mutley Plain to Hender's Corner and Crownhill, down through Manadon. Crownhill was a village. Honicknowle was a village. St. Budeaux was built and Crownhill going out towards St. Budeaux a few houses, but not like there are now. That's where most of the housing estates have been built, at Honicknowle or Ernesettle, Efford, Eggbuckland, and Plymouth, I would think, doubled in size after the housing estates were built. There was one housing estate that was built before the war in 1938 at Efford, and it was called the White City. People had been taken from their homes in the Barbican out to the first council house estate at Efford. They were forcibly taken from the Barbican, from New Street, and all those very old houses. No building went on during the war, but after the war, even though my grandmother's house was still standing, it was condemned. A lot of houses were condemned as being unfit for use, and those tenants were the first ones to be re-housed. My grandmother was one of them, and the first council estate that I can remember, and I think I'm right, is the old Efford estate, which takes in most of Blandford Road and Pike Road. The second one was Honicknowle and then they started extending further out, so Southway eventually – all council estates. A lot of people had been able to buy their houses after the war but they were all council houses. We had a lot of prefabs in Plymouth and they were gorgeous. People wanted a prefab because you not only had your wonderful kitchen, you had a refrigerator, you had a proper bathroom, and you had all the mod cons that most of the older houses didn't have. I know when I was evacuated we didn't have anything down in Cornwall. I'd already lived in a railway house my father was granted in Efford Lane, where we had all this electric and gas and a bathroom with a bath, so I really missed all that down in Cornwall. I just wondered where on earth I was! But they accepted it all down there because these little hamlets had never known any different.

We had some sympathy after the war, because a lot of the

German and Italian prisoners-of-war were decent people, we even used to mingle with Italian POWs in the city centre – they had patches on their arms for identification. In fact a few of my friends from school married Germans who had stayed on in Plymouth after the war, because they had chosen to stay in England. One became a green-grocer who, when I was married and living in Hooe, used to serve me vegetables, and he was a lovely man! So really any sympathy came after the war.

Music was alive in the war – it was what kept everybody going. It was a social thing, people had their radios on – *The Light Programme* – it always had music of the day. Many, many songs were written per week in the War. It was very important, and it kept people together. It kept people lively. It kept people from thinking too much about what may happen that evening if there was an air-raid. They sang during the air-raids. It was music that kept everybody together. Everybody knew the titles of the tunes and the words. Popular songs were: '*Kiss Me Goodnight, Sergeant Major*', '*The White Cliffs of Dover*', '*Coming in on a Wing of a Prayer*', '*The Siegfried Line*' and '*A Nightingale Sang in Berkeley Square*' which is a beautiful tune all about Berkeley Square, and sweethearts going there and being together at a quiet time – quiet enough to hear a nightingale sing – probably on a weekend. They used to get a forty-eight hour pass just for the weekend, and, if they were in London, they would probably end up in Berkeley Square.

Music was a paramount part of my childhood and these songs have stayed with me for years. When I have played piano sing-alongs to older people, even those with dementia, they come alive! The war-time spirit was all good natured and it really taught me how to get on with people. I always feel privileged to have lived through those years, they were hard years but it was a privilege, and I wouldn't have missed it for the world.

Elsie Hobbs

Image: Fotonow

Frederick Francis Alfred Brimacombe, born in Plymouth:

I was born at 16, The Parade, on the Barbican and I am 87 years old. We played cricket on The Parade on the Barbican, where they used to put their sails and fix all their gear, and the water cart used to come along there and get filled up with water, every day, from a great big stand pipe with a bend in it that fitted over the tank. It was horse-drawn and he would turn it on and fill up the tank and then go round to the different houses – you didn't get piped water – and sell it to them like that. We also had a guy coming round selling us rock salt from a hand-cart, and he had a rusty old saw, and he would cut you off a chunk of it. You didn't have fridges in those days, so you used the rock salt to preserve the stuff! Yes, cod and such would have the rock salt on it, and then be dried in the wind. The rock salt used to cure it and then the day before we were getting the fish ready to eat, we'd put it in a bowl of water and leave it there for twelve hours, then change the water and leave for another six hours, and change the water again…and then it was ready for you to eat!

My dad was a fisherman all the family had been – grandfather, great grandfather…and my earliest memory…well going to sea with my dad I guess. He had a boat called the *Perilla*, she was fifty feet and she worked four hands. I was just coming up to nine.

Father decided he was going to go out and hawk these fish, because the prices we were getting were terrible – a chunk of good, large whiting, 1 shilling and 6 for three stone we were getting! People didn't want it. We couldn't get outlets for it, not like today where you have outlets all over the world. So Father decides he is going to do fish-hawking, and he gets this cart and buys a horse from Gill's Yard in Vauxhall Street, and he didn't know it but it was the first time the horse had been put between shafts. He was going up Saltash Street and the horse saw a reflection of itself in the window of the *50 Shilling Tailors* and he just went straight through the window…they had to put it down…so that was the end of his fish-hawking.

Father was a hard working guy, when the fish got that people didn't want it he got a job with the Post Office as a linesman, he being able to do different types of knots with rope and that, he was with the GPO for about five or six years and then he went into the Dockyard as a rigger but he came out during the war years, came out of the Dockyard, and went on board a boat called the *Isobel* which was an old French boat that had come over from France during the occupation, and they got it up to Salcombe, and she filled up with water, and a guy called Arthur Easton bought her and fixed her up…

We had a 500lb unexploded bomb drop on The Parade there, *right* in front of our house – broke all the windows! Number 16, you can see where it landed now, they haven't changed the paving slabs, they are a different colour – a grey colour – to the rest, right opposite number 16, which is a pub now. Once I actually picked up a live incendiary bomb, over by The Three Crowns pub. It had come out of the aircraft and hit not the down pipe, but the shooting that goes along the front of the building. It must have caught the corner piece and that had broken its fall as it fell down and of course me, like an idiot, I picked it up! I had a cousin who had come down from Lowestoft, just joined the Navy, and he said, 'Gosh! That would look nice on the mantelpiece wouldn't it?' So I took it home to Dad but he said, 'Get rid of it! Chuck it overboard!' So I took it down again and threw it away. It's lucky it didn't go off.

During the war people had a comradeship feeling. If you ran out of bread, you said to 'Mrs Jones', 'I've run out of bread', and she would say, 'Here! Have half of what I have got!' That's the way it was on the Barbican; the Barbican was a village in itself really. We had a post office, a ships' chandler, baker, butcher, an engineer, the dress shop for children for shawls etc, two butchers and there were three fish shops, believe it or not, in Southside Street, one was *Mr Spry*...I can't remember the others. In the Sound you had *HMS Implacable*, *HMS Newcastle* and one other ship. Then you had Drake's Island covered in guns. The *Implacable* was an ex-French battle ship – they cleared everything off her deck, flattened her right out, and they put ack-ack guns on her and she was moored just by the breakwater fort. They had the breakwater fort loaded with guns as well, and when you stepped out of your front door to see what was going on, you could see the aircraft, the search lights on the aircraft, and the ack-ack guns having a go at them...the noise was just as if the gun was right beside you. The rattle of the guns was horrendous.

Frederick Brimacombe

Image: Fotonow

George Edward Easton, born 1920, in Catherine Street, Barbican, Plymouth:

My name is George Edward Easton and I was born at number 7, Catherine Street, Plymouth – the building has been pulled down now and there are new houses built there since 1945. My work pre-war, when I did start work, I worked for a small firm in Rendle Street, Plymouth as an errand boy and warehouse boy, and then as a seaman on a private yacht. I was also from a fishing family and occasionally I worked on one of the family boats; fishing, herring-catching…then I managed to get a job on a private schooner yacht as an able seaman, which, to me at that time, was a really good job – I learned most of my seamanship there. Then I joined the Naval Reserves and when the War started I was in active service – the Royal Navy.

My mother – this is a bit of history as it was before I was born – she worked in a firm called Rundle, Rogers and Brook. It was a tailoring firm and they tailored Service uniforms, and it was called the Britannia Works, in was in a street near Alton Street where they had their place of clothing; Navy, Army badges and gunnery badges, torpedo badges and things appertaining to the Royal Navy which was designed with stripes in gold and others in red…that sort of thing. That's where my mother came from and she was a really good Christian church-goer. She insisted myself and my brothers join St Saviour's Church. St Saviours church is on the top of Lambhay Hill and of course there is a story about that during the war… My schooling was…as an infant I went to Catherine Street

School which I well remember, the time I was in infant's school, and from there to juniors school which was St Andrews and that was quite near St Andrews Church.

When I was 22 years old in 1942, and the raids started early, at about 8 in the evening, and everybody would be down in the air-raid shelter, which was the basement of the house I lived in.

Interviewer: How many people would there have been?

About twenty of us tenants down there. When the war started Plymouth City Council, or some authority, put a steel plate over the whole ceiling with tubular uprights, like scaffolding poles, several of them all around to hold the plate up to the ceiling, it was fastened there so if you had a direct hit – if rubble would fall down – you would be safe. The only thing is if a bomb exploded then it would kill everyone there, especially with a steel plate. The concussion would have been terrible, but it was never bombed like that. We never had a direct hit. I believe it was the city council that established the Air Raid Wardens, and they were civvies, and they had a wide band around their arm with 'ARP Warden' marked on it, and they had the authority to order you. If the siren had gone, most people would naturally run, but there were people who wouldn't want to go until they heard the aircraft coming right over, but the wardens would say, 'You get in there!' And they would direct, or escort, you to the nearest air-raid shelter; there were various air-raid shelters in the streets. They spoke with authority. They were so authoritative they sounded more like policemen

– as if they had powers of arrest.

Interviewer: What did you do during a raid?

I couldn't do anything, but after about hour and a half to two hours, the German aircraft were coming to Plymouth from the east, and they were flying over us and they were releasing their bombs – the bomber is travelling at about 200mph – they release the bomb, and that bomb is travelling forward at the same speed as the aircraft, and then it gradually loses speed, but it is still dropping all the time. The Germans were extremely good at that. When the noise ceased I thought, 'I'll just go out for a breath of fresh air' so I got out and walked around – everything quiet – and I passed my church, St Saviour's on Lambhay Hill, and smoke was coming out of it, and I thought, 'Blimey! That's incendiaries they dropped there...' and there were bits of incendiaries that expended themselves – they were about *that* wide and about *that* long...

Interviewer: that's about 2 feet by 1 inch?

Yes, there were pieces of them about, and some had gone through the church roof, and I guessed the church was on fire inside but saw no flames anywhere. So first thing I thought, 'I will fetch the fire brigade', but you couldn't fetch the fire brigade because they weren't allowed out while the air-raid was on, and the policemen were not allowed out either. You see these films nowadays where they are squirting water on the fires, and that, but that was after the all clear. I tried to kick the door open, but it was very strong and I couldn't open it. The vicar was not the vicar I grew up with – he had only been given the parish about a year or two ago, and I hadn't even spoken to him because I was away most of the time. I was wondering, 'Should I call in?' The vicarage was adjoining the church. Then I thought, 'No' the vicarage was in darkness, I thought, 'He is probably in his shelter, where he is supposed to be.' He had two boys – younger than me. I knew if I could have got in there I could have helped and done something. I felt really helpless.

Later the aircraft came back again and there were more aircraft coming in, so of course I had to go back to the shelter, and then after about another hour or more, at about 3 or 4 in the morning the all clear went. I went to bed and my brothers…they weren't in the Army then, it was before they were conscripted…they came into me shouting – and I *knew*. I couldn't help it, there was a raging fire in the church and the church was gone, and I wished to hell that the fire brigade could have got there and saved it. They did come after the all-clear. But don't ring them, because they are not allowed…any more than we are…they have to take cover – that was an awful thing. I was ready…I would have volunteered for the fire service in a minute, because it was my church.

George Easton

Image: Fotonow

Harold Edward Perry, born 1930, in St Paul Street, Stonehouse, Plymouth:

Emma Place, in Stonehouse, played a very important part in my childhood. In 1940, when I was ten, we heard air-raids going on. As children we used to help people dig out their gardens to put air-raid shelters up and we'd fill up sandbags. We got used to hearing the air-raid sirens going on, and the all clear going off, after. I suppose from '39 to '40 it was reasonably quiet. But in 1940, I think, they dropped the first bomb in Swilly (North Prospect) and I think there were two or three people killed there at that time – that was an eye-opener to us. It was just random bombing, nothing specific, just random; blanket bombing. Then on the 12th September 1940, a bomb dropped up at the top of Chapel Street, which was almost on the corner of Emma Place. Typical of all children back in that time, we'd go looking for shrapnel – parts of the bomb – as souvenirs, even though the place was roped off with signs, 'Danger!' 'Do Not Enter!' This bomb was devastating – it had hit a fish & chip shop full blast, and thirteen people were blown to bits – five marines and seven civilians. I can only just talk about this now – I couldn't talk about it before. When I went on to this bomb-site looking for shrapnel I came across a body part of a Marine...I knew it was a Marine because of the serge uniform he had on...anyway that upset me, obviously. To be honest about it, I put it at the back of my mind, as if it didn't exist, but it has never, ever left me. I can still picture Emma Place as it was – right opposite the chip shop was a church, St George's church with steps going

up and a big old-fashioned lamp over the top of it, old
wrought iron with a big lamp coming down. A couple of
doors up from that was a sweet shop – I always used to
see toffees on plates and little toffee hammers with them.
There was a town hall, that was burnt out in the end, with
a Naval prison down below and they'd march them up
there, faces scraping the floor, or their gas mask hitting
them. I remember the women from the council estate,
would come out, batting hell out of these Naval Patrol
men, trying to get them to release them! It certainly made
you very street-wise. And right across the road from the
sweet shop was Mr Coles, the tobacconist; he had retired
from the Navy, and also lived in our house. Durnford
Street was called Chapel Street back in those days. I
would take my sister to a Stonehouse picture house in
Union Street called *The Grand*, and when people walked
out, we would walk in and sit in their seats – we got away
with it! I would watch a serial every week, I wouldn't miss
it...Flash Gordon and his Trip to Mars or Larry Trent on
Treasure Island. Union Street was a mile long, with a pub
nearly on every corner, they reckoned. People would start
their night in a pub at one end and then try to get to the
other end! Vivid memories...

Interviewer: Tell me a bit about food, what did you like?
Was your mother a good cook?

My mum was a lovely cook, really. In the early days, I
told you we would have whatever we could afford to
buy, really. Most times it was fish, mackerel, they'd come
round the door with mackerel you see, on a handcart.
They would gut it for you and take the heads off. Mum

would clean it, and that's what we would have most times, that was oily fish, which is good for you anyway; we still eat a lot of fish now. I can never, ever remember tasting poultry, not until I was sixteen or seventeen and my dad bought home a goose for Christmas after the war, and that was the first time I remember tasting it. We never tasted beef, or meat, back in that time, but we used to have rabbit. Believe you me, rabbit is gorgeous to eat! My mum and dad used to go down to King Street where there used to be loads of hand-carts selling goods. There used to be a railway arch there, years ago, and they'd all be lined along the pavement, and if it was an evening they'd hang oil lamps up. It always looked nice, and you could always buy a cheap cut of meat, or something, there. But never do I remember tasting poultry! In a butcher's down Union Street the rabbits would be hanging up on a rail, all skinned, and Mum would make pies – it's a gorgeous bit of meat. We couldn't get eggs because of the rationing, so we'd have powdered eggs. Spam which was 'Specially Preserved American Meat' we used to have, and corned beef. We never saw a banana. The Japanese confiscated everything.

The Dockyard gates were locked when the siren sounded, and no-one could go in or out until the all clear sounded. We never had an air-raid shelter at that time, so we'd go under the table. We had black-out blinds with tape on the windows in case there were blasts, and we always left the front door open, so if there was a bomb blast it would go right through the house and wouldn't blow your door off. Believe you me – it was very, very frightening. As a child your imagination is all over the place – if you imagine the fiercest thunder and lightening you've ever heard, and magnify that several times – well that is what the effect would be. You'd hear the bombs drop and feel the ground tremor that came with it and you'd say a prayer, *It won't be us, it won't be us...* First you'd get a fast German plane come over, could be a fighter, and he would drop a load of flares over the area that's got to be bombed, which would be the city centre, then the bombers would come in with their incendiary bombs and drop them – they reckon there was a quarter million incendiaries dropped on Plymouth through the war. The incendiaries were phosphorus, so whenever they exploded, it would spray out, and catch whatever it touched on fire. Then they came over with the heavy bombers that were able to pick out where they wanted to drop the bombs. The city centre was annihilated.

Only a mile from the city centre, halfway up Union Street, there was a bomb dropped somewhere where the town hall would have been, and it blew all our windows out; the plaster came off our ceilings and walls. My sister screamed, she was a bundle of nerves – we all were – and she ran out of the house in a panic. Luckily somebody grabbed her and pulled her into a doorway. The sky was ablaze with searchlights, tracer bullets, fire-bombs, and not knowing my sister was safe, we ran looking for her past my cinema, right down to the Royal Naval Barracks. There were big hollows in the wall there, where they'd made air-raid shelters for the people. You'd go in there and pray to God it wouldn't hit you, there were so many people in there – it would take the lot, which it did up in Portland Square… We found her outside a shop with the person who'd helped her, and we all came back home. It was in quite a state at home, and the gas and electricity was lost for maybe ten days. Your first thoughts are of getting a meal together. A few doors up was a man called Miller whose parents had a range stove which they kept on the go constantly – to keep the people of East Street in meals of some sort. We also used our boy-scout methods, we made holes in a biscuit tin with a few candles, put the lid on to trap the heat in and eventually it would cook something up – even if it took all day! You had to do these things.

After that it was so bad that we couldn't take any more chances, so we went to Union Street – to The Odeon cinema which was beside the railway bridge that went over to Millbay Station – and from there we hitched lifts out of Plymouth. Lots of people did this; there were lorries, and the drivers would take people wherever they were going – Cornwood, Plympton, wherever…you never knew. My mum had a friend in Federation Road, Laira, that she thought would take us in – lots of people were very kind taking people in – so we went up there, my mum, my sister and me onto her doorstep, and asked if we could stay, but she wouldn't take us in, even for the night. So then we had to walk down a long road, past the church (where Joan and I got married actually) to an allotment where my granddad had a shed, and that is where we spent the next couple of nights. And it was damn cold. It was March! But we felt safe there. I must mention a Mr & Mrs Garrard who lived in Underwood in Plympton, they had three children of their own, but they let us sleep sometimes on the floor in their living room. We were forever grateful to them for that.

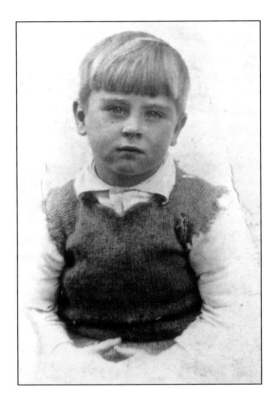

Harold Perry, aged 3,
at St Paul's Street School, Stonehouse, 1933.

Harold Perry

Image: The Word Machine

Jack (John) Dennis Berryman, born 1927, at 2, Osborne Place, The Hoe, Plymouth:

Interviewer: Can you tell me where you were when the German invasion of Poland was announced?

I was twelve years old. I was at home, and on the radio, at 11 o'clock, we heard Neville Chamberlain speak. He had given Germany a time limit to withdraw from Poland. Never got any response and the Germans, of course, did not withdraw. I think his words were, '…consequentially, I have to inform you that this country is now at war with Germany.' We weren't bothered. When I say 'we' I mean people I knew. We were so confident of victory – we really were – and of course Plymouth was a great Naval port, we had the RAF sea-planes at Mountbatten and we had various Army and Royal Marine bases, so we were a very military town, and there was no doubt at all we would win. I then went down to Tinside for a swim! But we boys did try to help, I belonged to a Boy Scout troop, and in the months that followed we did two things in our puny effort to help the war effort! One was going around door to door with a great big cart collecting newspaper. We would take the newspapers to Millbay Station, which was then in use as a railway station. We would sell the newspapers there and put the money into the Spitfire Fund. We all understood that a Spitfire in those days cost £5,000. Churchill bought over a wonderful Canadian industrialist called Beaverbrook and put him in charge of aircraft production, and I think in due course we were manufacturing more planes than the Germans. So, we Boy Scouts would go out onto the pavements and beg for money from people passing by…just a small amount… then we'd place the money in a line on the pavement – say someone had given us a penny – and then if someone gave a threepenny bit then that took up three penny spaces, a sixpence – six spaces – a shilling, in those days – twelve spaces – and so forth but we were only asking for little amounts, and we would try to make the line of coins as long as possible, and that money would go into the Spitfire Fund! It was great fun.

Interviewer: Can you tell me a little about your friends and then your memories of the Blitz?

We were all keen on sports; at Hoe Grammar school it was soccer, hockey and cricket. At Plymouth College it was rugby, hockey and cricket. We all liked tennis down at West Hoe, and other places in Plymouth. For just for a penny, or tuppence, you could rent a court to play. So when the weather was appropriate we would often play tennis. We also liked swimming and most of us had a season ticket at Tinside, that was admission to the pool and the changing rooms there. So we had these athletic activities. I often went to the pier – it was very good. If you walked along the pier there were steps to the left, which led to diving platforms that the Leander Swimming Club used. At the entrance to the pier there were lots of slot machines, a penny a go. One could walk the length of the pier and there was a dance hall, a circular dance hall at the end, which was very popular on Saturday nights. My younger sister…she was older than me but younger to Margaret…she met her husband there. People would go on the pier, it would cost you a penny I think, and there were places there from which you could swim and fish.

My memories of the Blitz are that it was terrifying. The first point is that Cherbourg is only ninety to a hundred miles from Plymouth, and so the *Luftwaffe* did not have far to come, and Plymouth had a great Naval base and its Dockyard would be making, manufacturing and repairing warships, so it was going to be a frequent target. The calamitous ones occurred on March 20th/21st 1941. I went to a Boy Scout first-aid lesson; this was in a side street off Union Street, near Stonehouse. One of my friends was lying flat on his back on a table and I was putting a splint on his left arm. All four of his limbs were in splints – and then the bombing started! We had to undo him very quickly and make our way – with the bombs coming down – to our respective homes. On another occasion – our house had a basement, a ground floor and I think three upper floors – the authorities said that our basement was bomb-proof. When the air-raid signals would go off sometimes people from the Hoe would come in to our basement to take shelter until the raid was over. One night a young man bought in a screaming young woman. They had been up on the Hoe, in darkness and she was screaming because of a splinter wound in her thigh. We couldn't get an ambulance, because there were so many casualties, until 5am. She was in the basement, poor girl, screaming her head off. The bombs were terrifying…they came…you could hear the whistling, and you weren't sure if they would land on you or not. Our house was a terraced house, and a house about eight houses away from us received a bomb. Opposite our house was the Hoe Bowling Green and the pavilion was burnt to a cinder. The Germans dropped a lot of incendiaries and in the March raid, the Hoe Grammar School, which was a wonderful school, was totally destroyed.

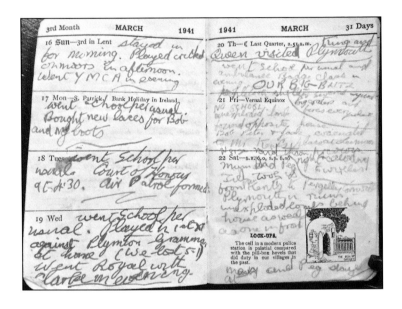

Pages from Jack Berryman's 1941 diary, when he was 14.

'20th *March: King and Queen visited Plymouth. OUR BIG Blitz. People took shelter, several injured. Big craters and fires everywhere.*

21st March: NO SCHOOL. Unexploded bomb found opposite house. Worse raid than previous night.

22nd March: Plymouth in ruins.'

Janet Rastan, born in Mannamead Road, Plymouth:

Interviewer: What do you remember about your home, and your neighbours?

Well, my parents rented a house in Peverell, somewhere. I remember the neighbours. There was a girl that was several years older than myself and I played with her, and there was a boy the other side who used to eat snails! I remember we had trams in Plymouth then, and I used to get into trouble for bowling my hoop along the tram-lines. I always remember waiting every night when it became dusk for the lamp-lighter to come along. I do remember the lamp-lighter, especially. That was a special moment in the day for me, because he would come along, with his long pole, and light the gas lamp in the street. And I remember a man coming along with a barrow with roast chestnuts, you know – with the little fire in it?

I remember going to the shop just along the road and buying a ha'p'orth of raspberry drops out of my pocket money. I used to get tuppence per week and if I spent it, then that was that! Mostly I bought raspberry drops, because I had a friend who was addicted to them, who lived somewhere around here. I remember saving up to give my mother a birthday present and I saved three weeks' pocket money – six old pence – and I managed to buy her a 'diamond' ring – made of glass – and I still had some money left over to buy a doll's feeding bottle! That was my sixpence spent. I used to get a comic that was tuppence a week called *Chick's Own*.

Interviewer: Were you and your family living in Plymouth

at any point during the war?

No, but I visited because I had grandparents here. I did visit quite regularly, but of course during the Blitz we went to Liskeard in Cornwall. My mother bought a cottage there and we had a huge amount of people coming to stay. If you had a bed, you gave it up to someone and while the Blitz was going on in Plymouth we had...I don't remember their names...possibly staying longer in this little cottage. I went to the local school there, the local Grammar school which was co-educational. I looked silly when I first went there because I was beautifully behaved, and stood up every time a teacher spoke to me, and of course I was a laughing stock because they didn't do that. They were more rough and ready, but great fun! And we had evacuees from all over the place. Two of my friends were billeted a farming family, and they were from the East End of London, and George, the boy, he became a professor later on. It gave him his chance in life because he had lived in the East End slums – his grandmother used to sit on the doorstep smoking a clay pipe!

One evacuee went back to her school in Kent, and went on to become the head of all the forensic work in Scotland Yard. She's retired now. She's a little bit older than I am. We had all sorts of people. I do remember a couple of Polish airmen. The authorities had come to our door and rung the bell and said, 'We've brought you some Poles.' My mother thought, 'Well, I don't want any poles...I have washing poles in the garden'. They were two men in the Polish Air Force – foreigners used to come over here and join our Forces. I remember one little girl with red hair, and every time the siren went she would scream, and scream, and scream because she had been in the bombing.

We used to sit in the cupboard under the stairs because we didn't have a shelter, and gradually we got a bit blasé. Sometimes I would go under the dining room table, but we would stay up in the bedroom much of the time when the Blitz was on in Plymouth, and we would watch Plymouth burning. All the windows would be rattling and shaking. You didn't know who was going to turn up and ask for a bed for the night. We all tried to help one another. We had odd raids, but where I was in Liskeard, Cornwall we didn't have any bombs dropping. Nevertheless, when a raid took place our windows used to shake and rattle although it was fifteen miles away, and you could see planes being shot down. The whole of Plymouth looked like it was on fire. It was dreadful.

When I was visiting my grandfather we used to go down into the cellar and I always remember wanting to sit next to the cellar door, by the opening to the garden, because I didn't want to be buried alive. I wanted an escape route. I think I must have had a good survival instinct! I did come back to Plymouth, to teach, later and I went to a very poor part of the town, and the headmistress of the infant school there had been bombed during the Blitz, and she had lost all three of her children. I thought it terribly brave of her to go back and look after other people's children.

Janet Rastan

Image: Fotonow

Jean Henrietta Hargraves, born 1932, lived at 17, Camden Street, North Hill, Plymouth:

There were five of us children at Camden Street. I think back now – how did we all manage? It wasn't a big house. The front room was not allowed to be used; it was kept for special. My gran and granddad lived upstairs, so it was a full house. I remember the authorities coming in and making an air-raid shelter in a room downstairs. It was a big room, no windows. I think it's where they kept coal and logs and that. They reinforced it, put little steps in, and put access in the pavement, so if we had a direct hit they could get us out. We practically lived in it when it got really bad. There was an oven to keep the pasties warm, and drinks and we slept in hammocks. The smaller children – I was next to the youngest – we just got put in the hammocks and slept.

Even when I was seventeen and a half I wasn't allowed out! I'll tell you what, I don't know how true this is mind you, but we had a mantlepiece and a fire, and there were about three shilling pieces on there to put in the meter – and nobody was allowed to touch those. My mother always said if we were invaded she was going to gas us. She was determined that the Germans wouldn't get hold of us. My mother used to love going out watching the aerial dogfights – and we didn't like that. I used to cry because I was frightened for her, but she loved it. I do remember one night – well it was early morning – do you remember them talking about 'Lord Haw-Haw'? I think his real name was Joyce. He used to come on the radio and say a place was going to be bombed; blood would be running...and all this and that. You know, like

'Tokyo Rose' when the Japanese were fighting. She used to come on and talk about what the Japanese were going to do. Well Lord Haw-Haw came on this time, and he said Portland Square was going to be bombed, and blood would be running and…you know…it was. My mother grabbed hold of us and we went over there to have a look. I like my bed and there we were running around Plymouth in the early hours of the morning…I don't think people could let it get to them. They just got on with it, for the best. I can remember grown-ups talking…I must have been earwigging…they said that Ebrington Street – there were two big underground shelters there – had a direct hit and there was nobody alive. My friend Sylvia, she went there, so when I went to school I *saw* Sylvia, and it was a bit of a shock you know. I said, 'I thought you were dead!' But it was so bad the warden wouldn't let her and her parents across to go in the shelter – he shoved them in the door out of the way.

I remember the end of the war – I really do. Sound asleep. Now I'm thirteen, a teenager and you know what teenagers are like – don't want to get out of bed, do they! Mother shaking me, 'Come on, get up!' Me saying, 'No, no not again!' and I can hear all this banging, and banging and I'm thinking, 'Oh God, they've all gone mad!' My mother took us all on the Hoe. The banging sound was men, they had dustbin-lids and were banging them – everybody went mad! Oh yes! They were burning everything up on the Hoe, anything they could get their hands on. I wanted to get back to bed – it was the middle of the night. They could have waited until the morning!

Jean Hargraves

Image: Fotonow

Joan Wills and Maureen Sawyer, cousins from Plymouth, lived in Manor Gardens:

Maureen: I must've been about nine… I remember being in bed with my siren-suit on and hearing the drone of planes and I remember feeling sick, and sometimes being sick, and I would cry. I can remember that. My gran would say, 'There's nothing to cry for, you're very safe.'

Interviewer: Did you feel like that as well, Joan?

Joan: I must have been afraid, but being older I would have been more frightened thinking, 'It's the end! I'm going to die!' – you know? Especially when we had to leave the shelter when it was bombed – that's when I felt fear. We lived in Octagon Cottages, off the Octagon on Union Street, where the Larry Speare shop is now, and our air-raid shelter was under where their car-park is now – I don't know if anybody else knows that? I was running across – I could hear the planes up there and the bombs were coming down – and then this sailor threw himself over me, to protect me, and then I lost my new hat – it was blown off – and he took me to another shelter... The next morning there were bodies on top of the shelter – they were covered over – it was people who'd been inside the shelter.

Interviewer: Was the sailor all right?

Both: Yes, yes.

Maureen: I remember distinctly when we went into the shelter there was an elderly sailor with a peaked cap and a beard. He used to always have sweets and would tell the children, 'Sit around!' and he would tell us stories, he kept a lot of kiddies happy. He was always there and because of his beard, we thought he might be God.

Joan: Every night, when we were expecting the Blitz, we'd walk out, or get lifts from Army lorries, to the country, to Plympton, and that's where we were eventually evacuated from. There was a school at Plympton, where were all laying down on – palliasses, are they called? Straw mattresses. Next morning these people were sitting over at a desk and called out all these different places where evacuees were welcome. We were very lucky because, with Gran's help, we ended up in Dartington…

Maureen: …In boarding houses. Park School was a big school, and we had a wonderful education there. There were just a few from Plymouth, the rest were from London. Joan was in the big house, called the Big House. There were three boarding houses, and myself and Joan's younger sister were there, with a youngster that lived near us, and Joan was in the Big House and we had House Mothers. My House Mother was called Mrs Tritty.

Joan: I can remember getting Red Cross parcels from America with clothing, sweets and big Canadian apples. We were *so* well fed! I liked my food and I learned to eat very quickly, because if you finished quickly you could go up for seconds. I used to burn my tongue many a time! Once a month we'd have a visit from Gran.

Maureen: I remember sitting on a lorry, crying my eyes out saying, 'I don't want to go, Gran! I don't want to go!' I can remember that … but I got accustomed to the school; I loved it. We used to have nature walks; we had nothing like that in Plymouth. Down through to the River Dart, we learned to swim in the River Dart – health and safety wouldn't allow it these days – it was grand, we were there for about four and a half years and we had a lovely time. Yes, when war started I was about nine and a half or ten, and I was sixteen when it finished. Joan was about ten.

Joan: We had a healthy life, we'd walk down to the River Dart, through the woods, and all you could smell was garlic and bluebells. Three mile walk, taking Marmite sandwiches, we still love Marmite don't we?!

Maureen: Oh yes, and every Sunday and once a month on a Saturday we had sixpence, and we'd walk into Totnes – to Woolworths – to spend our sixpence. We'd buy sweets then walk back again, everything was walk then, you know?

Interviewer: Did you have any connection with the people of Dartington after you left?

Maureen: Many years ago we went back, Park School it was called then, the Big House was still there – as a school, someone came out of the school and asked what we were doing…we explained and they said, 'Come in! We're just having a lesson on the War!' So we were standing in front of them answering their questions on the war! Someone asked if we knew Hitler! We were taken aback…we must have looked ancient to him!

Interviewer: What were peoples' spirits like after the war?

Maureen: Oh, cheerful! Absolutely marvellous and everybody was your friend, everybody helped each other, anyone did anything for Gran – and you'd do anything for one another. She could always borrow a cup of milk, or sugar, tea...if you were on rations, and the rations were so little...

Interviewer: I get the impression there was a lot of excitement about the new town going up?

Joan: Yes, yes, I think Dingles was the first up. Because we came from such a poor background, Dartington was our idea of heaven; we couldn't have picked anything better than that.

Maureen: We really were extremely lucky, we can't say anything else. We had a better life than millions of others and I think too that those people from London and Gravesend appreciated it too, because their lives were much worse than ours.

Kenneth Bonning, born 1938, Queen Alexandra Nursing Home, Devonport, Plymouth:

Interviewer: Can you give me memories of the Blitz?

Yes! It was terrifying! They put an Anderson shelter in our garden at 27, Albert Place, Devonport, and every night we had to go down there and it was just terrifying. My father had joined the Ambulance Service and was out driving an ambulance because he was one of the few people in Devonport who had a licence – he was too old to be taken into the Navy – he joined in 1942. One night I remember Mother carrying me in her arms down to the shelter, and I looked up to see the search lights in the sky and picked out a plane in the sky...then we came out of the shelter to find our home was gone.

It was your childhood, your growing up time so you accepted everything that was going on, although you were apprehensive all the time. There was a pair of ornamental dogs that had belonged to my granddad, which we managed to dig out of the rubble, that's all we had left – along with a barometer. There were a lot of looters. A lot of stuff was stolen.

My mother used to bring home snoek and whale-meat and make pies. It tasted fishy, difficult for a child to eat that sort of stuff...but we ate what we could get and were grateful for it. A boat came over from the West Indies with bananas, our first banana! My first ice-cream was down in Liskeard...they had no wafers to go with it so they put it between digestive biscuits. It was good – a real treat!

Interviewer: Did you leave the city because of the danger?

Yes, we had to. My father had joined the Navy, and the bombs came down and blew our house to bits. My mother had no money, so she walked with me from Plymouth to Brixham! That's where she came from – so we walked there. It took us two and a half days to walk to Brixham (about forty miles). She put me in a pram, with a few possessions, and we walked to Brixham. We stayed with my grandparents there. They were fishermen, and they were poor as church mice so they had no money.

The Government gave out billeting money, for staying with people, but because my father was self-employed before the war, we weren't entitled. Mother then had to find a job. A family called Mr and Mrs Wood took us in. He was an old Africa-hand, and his walls were covered with spears and shields and things like that, which I found particularly scary. He was a nice old fella, but the house was sort of scary with the shields, masks and spears plastered all over the wall.

Interviewer: Were you aware of what was going on in Europe as a whole?

Well – the fact that Hitler was everywhere! We were quite scared about the parachutists that were coming down – we used to keep a broom handle in the cupboard with a knife tied on the end. Mother said, 'If the buggers come down I'm gonna get them!' We thought they were coming! They destroyed Plymouth, our house and our business.

Interviewer: How did your new home compare to your old home during the war?

The ones we lived in during the war weren't our own homes, my mother worked for other people, we were live-in servants really, so it was quite restrictive where you could go. The lady who owned the house – I never spoke to her – she was that aloof. She gave my mother a hard time. In the mornings at 9 o'clock we had to go in with her, she sat on a seat and there was an old butler, who could have been a character out of a film – and a couple of old gardeners that she had – we would go in there, me and my mother, we'd have to stand up when she came in, and she would sit down and then we'd listen to the news at 9 o'clock in the morning. And there was news at 9 o'clock at night. I was asleep by then, but my mother had to go in and listen to the news with her. There were some soldiers billeted on her – they were from up on the hill behind us – it had a gun on it. But she said, 'They are not to come in the house.' My mother had to take cans of food out to the chap who wasn't allowed to cross the threshold. A soldier had to come down, pick it up and take it up to the others, they weren't allowed in the house!

Also, people were invited to give up their saucepans for Spitfires. Everybody gave up saucepans, and my mother approached this old lady to give up saucepans and she said, 'How will I entertain the Germans if they come?' That was the first time I realised there was a difference – normal, ordinary people would give up as much as they could to sustain the nation, but there was a class of people who would not. It was my first introduction to Socialism.

Interviewer: What was the atmosphere of your neighbour-hood like after the war?

Great! Well we were boys, weren't we! We could run around all the bombed buildings, it was everything a boy could want! I had a bike, I could go out fishing, I could go anywhere... My mother would pack me off with a sandwich and I'd go away and then come back when the sun went down. We had freedom – as children we were free! I used to make airplanes, go to pictures... Fabulous.

Interviewer: What did you think of the re-building?

Well, they knocked down some nice places...things happened in Plymouth. All of a sudden they knocked it down and tried to make it a square layout – like America – that was a bit sad really. They should have kept all the nice buildings in Plymouth like the Corn Exchange, the Guinness Clock...they cut Ebrington Street in half. Bedford Street was a nice street, but it all had to go, and I can't understand why. Even the Pannier Market was attractive. I remember going to see the first escalator in Dingles – we called it the 'moving stairs' – and going up and down there thirty or forty times! There was new technology coming all the time. My chum, the chap who lived next door to us in Gordon Terrace, he came out of the Navy and joined the Corporation as a steam-roller driver – they were rolling out the new roads and he had a big steam-roller. I used to sit up there with him, riding along, as he was working! Things were changing, inno-vation was happening, rationing was finishing and they were knocking down buildings and putting up new ones.

Kenneth Bonning

Image: Fotonow

Linda James, born in Plymouth, 1944:

My eldest brother was born in 1946. I had another brother born eight years after me, and a sister sixteen years after me. So my youngest brother and sister know hardly anything of the life my brother and I had in Plymouth when we were children, and what our parents and grandparents did – their life was so different. When my younger brother Derek was born, in 1952, he grew up as life was getting better and we had moved to a council house at Manadon, that was like a palace compared to the flat that my eldest brother and I lived in with my mother and father! It was off St Peter's Road, in one of the first houses they built in that area, and it was unbelievable – we had our own bathroom with our own toilet! Hot running water all the time…and a huge garden…until they built on the end of it. We were a long way from our school, but as we wanted to stay at Hyde Park we used to walk to the Golden Hind pub and catch a bus from there, so that was an adventure in itself.

During the bombings a lot of people went outside the city at night, to places like Cornwood, to be safe. My mother was in the Auxiliary Fire Service and she worked in the Fire Station up at Greenbank. She did the 'plotting', as you see in the films, to say where the bombs were falling. She said they often had bombs falling around them, and sometimes they had to get under a big metal table that was there for protection. One time her boss said, 'Come on Sally – underneath the table!' but he pushed her and her friend so hard to get under it – to keep them safe – she was badly bruised down her side and on her shoulder and her friend received a black eye – but he was afraid they would be hit. Fortunately there wasn't a direct hit. She lodged with her best friend's aunty in Ladysmith Road at that time, and often after doing night duty they'd go up on the Hoe to relax for a smoke, and a breath of fresh air before they went home. She said that once she saw Mount Edgecumbe house burning – all lit up. She was actually dancing on Plymouth pier the night before it was bombed. She said dancing was one of the few things they had left to do – dancing or go to the cinema.

When we were small and Mother wasn't working, we used to go to the Belgrave cinema on Mutley Plain, and the Forum at Devonport and sometimes the State at St Budeaux, depending on which films were being shown. I remember we'd line up outside the cinema at 12 o'clock, with our pasties in grease-proof paper bags that we'd bought for sixpence each at Ivor Dewdney's in King Street. Sometimes Mum would bring a thermos of tea. One day we enjoyed watching *Robin Hood*, starring Richard Todd, so much that we stayed and sat all through the second showing, and then Mum said, 'Shall we see it again? Dad'll be coming out of work by then so we can go home with him!' So we watched it again – three showings! My mother used to love Fred Astaire and Ginger Rogers, and all those films that would take you out of your bit of hardship, for a time, and we just loved it. So we'd watch a film and then walk home. In those days everybody could smoke inside, so you'd come out smelling like a kipper! You'd always try to sit at the back, because if you sat too near the front you'd hurt your eyes.

Maggie Daniels, born and grew up in Oreston, Plymouth:

I suppose I was about two when the war started. I remember my mother picking me up during an air-raid – my father had built a shelter in the garden. I remember being taken down there and my mother going to get my brother, who was six years older than me. I can remember tins of Smiths Crisps all lined up, with their little packets of blue salt, in this air-raid shelter, and all the neighbours would come pouring in. One thing that has stayed in my mind forever was when I was playing with some friends I had, and we fell out. I said to them, 'I'm never going to speak to you again!' That night a bomb fell on their house, and the whole family was wiped out. I can remember my mother saying to me, 'You should never, ever say anything you're going to regret.' That's stuck forever – that stays with me.

I remember the oil tanks burning at Turnchapel for several days, three, four days even longer it could have been. I remember the bombs coming down, you could hear the sirens going off and you'd think, 'Oh gosh!' and you might be out playing with friends, and their mothers would hide you under their stairs, or under the kitchen table – not that it would have done a lot of good if a bomb had a direct hit, but I suppose it protected us from falling glass and falling debris. One fell in our garden. We had a fish-pond and I remember going out the next morning, the windows were all blown in and all the fish were laying dead – all scattered all over the garden.

I remember having all my clothes made out of my father's cast-off shirts and jackets; I had a little skirt that had been made out of his jacket, and probably a blouse made out of an old shirt! I went to Oreston Village School and if the sirens went off, there was an air-raid shelter behind the school in the field and we all went in there and stayed put until the all clear went. It was quite nice to get out of lessons – it was always quite exciting. Oreston was virtually a village in those days, the whole Plymstock area wasn't developed. It was very much a social life in the village. My father and grandfather were builders. My father built a lot of Oreston and a lot of the houses over at Hooe, and of course the bombed houses – he had to put them back up again. And he used to run the ferries that went from Oreston to Turnchapel to Plymouth – of course a lot of their boats were carted off across the channel to France during the war. I remember the trains going from Oreston into Friary Station. Mother and I used to catch them quite often and walk the rest of the way into Plymouth and get a pasty. We'd queue up for everything. I do remember going shopping for a jelly, I don't think it was in Plymouth, with my very old school friend who I'd known since I was four, and we were queuing up for jellies and you were only allowed one jelly, and I think it was June's mother who said, 'Put our hats on!' Because all the mother's wore hats in those days. So June and I put our mothers' hats on, and *we* went in and queued up and got another packet of jelly! I think it was a simpler way of life back then in those days. You didn't expect to have everything immediately.

Maggie Daniels

Image: Fotonow

Margaret Blanche Webb, née Gliddon, born 18th December, 1917 at 5, Victoria Street, Plymouth:

My dad had ambitions. So when he was in the Navy, my mum took a shop. There were two markets in Plymouth before the war. There was quite a big one – the Meat Market – on one side, all covered. The stalls had shop fronts to show their meats. Of course there was no re-frigeration in those days. I don't remember how many stalls were there but it was a big covered market, and it had inspectors. On the other side, also covered, was the Vegetable Market, which was the same size, and in between the two markets there were two rows of shops and that was called Market Avenue. I think our shop was number 5. There were, maybe, twenty shops each side and they were all different. Both markets had four en-trances, the shops on one side – they were pianos, and music…and the other side there was a jewellers, and next door to that was our shop and it was a restaurant as well. We also sold our produce. Next to us was a sweet shop; the owner had a brother called Alan… I remember a big china shop, and another one sold pictures. There were two butchers, one was called Parsons and the other was called Merraford, but they were outside the main market. Our family restaurant was named Gallagher's… I could, given time, remember all of them… There was a chemist at the bottom of the other side – they were very good – called 'Fernley Wallis' – she was a matron in the hospitals, but she gave that up to work in the shop. There wasn't much to be had really; you didn't see bananas or oranges. You may see a couple of English apples, which weren't any good. We were fortunate really, my dad didn't want to pay Corporation rent; he wanted to get his own place. He worked out that Plymouth could only expand to the north. So we went out to live in West Park. Well, it wasn't called that then, it came under Plympton, not Plymouth. Our house was old but we had electric light! Dad did all the electrics himself, burying the cables in 18-inch thick walls – he was exceptionally clever. When we went out to the new place there was a builder chap there called Holmes, and he was starting to build at West Park, but he couldn't get anyone in the houses until he had got people in running the four shops he'd also built, so we took one and went from having a restaurant to being a greengrocer's shop! I think this was in 1938, or about twelve months before the war started. Dad got hold of a van and took the windows out and the sides off to make it into a travelling shop! We stocked it every night with apples and oranges, all the fruit on one side and all the veg on the other, and we did that all through the war. Vegetables were hard to come by but Dad knew a farmer, up in Exmouth, I think. He used to grow veg. One time Mum bought a whole field of cabbages! It was up behind where Coombe Park Road was, I don't know if the field's still there now – that was a terrible winter. We were lucky in that dad got the contract to serve all the military places and also all the forts – which were all in use in those days.

The war didn't start right away, we had a phoney war; nothing happened for twelve months while Germany was stringing Churchill along. I used to go dancing and during the war everything was flattened, so I could leave home in West Park and be in the Duke of Cornwall, or the Guildhall – which was a favourite because they had a ball every month which was only sixpence – or on the pier, in half an hour – just walking, because there were so many short cuts where buildings had been, and I never got accosted once. I was married in the May of 1938, and by October my husband been called up, he was already in the Fire Service but they still called him up. He was called William. Before we married, he lived in number 20, How Street. There was only one bedroom, which his mother and father had, leaving him and his sister in the only other room. There wasn't a front room. He had a chair to sleep in and she had a bed. He'd never slept in a bed until he married me! At our wedding reception, we had a long table in our restaurant where all the guests were sat and in those days you didn't have wedding receptions in restaurants; you had them in your front room. It was a lovely day.

After working in Bristol and Weston-Super-Mare I managed to get back to Ernesettle in Plymouth where I trained with the Navy to make shells for submarines. Large ones right down to the two pounders. I was on permanent nights again... But after my training I came out as Senior Inspector. And where I worked it is still the same today – there's a long path to go down to get to it. When you go over the Tamar Bridge look down to your left, you'll see the path going in... Inside the tunnel, they'd built concrete rooms, each separated from the other so if one blew up they didn't all go. A train ran around the back of the rooms bringing the work for the day, or the night. There would be about sixteen or eighteen women working on this. It was such a dangerous job – handling gunpowder, and the cordite was a bit like varying lengths of spaghetti, and thin or fat, depending on what type of shells or torpedoes you were filling. We had to have exact measurements of everything – like the gunpowder – and you used maybe half a dozen silken ties, depending on the plan you had. Everything had to be absolutely spot on, and I, as Inspector, had to put my seal on it, so I had to be absolutely sure they were right. One of the rooms blew up down there, it received a direct hit, but not all the rooms went because of the walls between them. We had three men working down with us. They used to rotate the train drivers. One of them was Eddie Earl, from the undertakers and none of them had been fit for war. I was about twenty-six, and I did enjoy it! All the girls were lovely and we all just lived for the day, you know?

Margaret Gliddon's Identity Card, dated 25ᵗʰ February, 1943.

Margaret Webb

Image: Fotonow

Maureen Baser grew up in Donegal Terrace, Stoke, Plymouth:

In 1943 when I was five and at school in Somerset Place, I can remember going to the air-raid shelter for the school, which was on Bunker's Hill – it's a very steep hill. I remember at home being taken down our shelter at night times and put to bed in the shelter. The grown-ups would drink tea and play cards all night, get up the next day and carry on as normal. I can remember incendiary bombs – we had a couple on our house, which my father made safe. My gran was an ARP warden and my father used to do firefighting. There was an orphanage at the top of Ford Hill, where the blocks of flats are now, and that went up one night – went up in flames. My mother and her sister went to the pictures one night, at The Palladium, at the bottom of Ford Hill. Her sister was heavily pregnant, and this was 1941 the night of the big raids. They were watching a cowboy film, and the banging they thought was part of the film, was actually a raid. When they came out of the cinema the bombs were falling, literally falling around them, and they had to come up Ford Hill running from doorway to doorway. I can remember going down to see a plane that had crash-landed down at Penlee Way. There used to be a big house there, a really grand resi-dence, and we went down to look at the crater that the plane had gone in.

With rationing my mother was quite 'in' with the butcher – so we did well. My grandfather worked as a cook at the hospital, so he always came home with extra food, and my father used to get food from the ships in the

Dockyard – the American ships that used to come in. I always remember the first white bread; he got that from the American ships and bought it home. White bread and chewing gum! It was something different, our bread was grey, unless you made your own, but this was white bread – it was quite an event! After the war I used to go swimming down at Mount Wise. One day I was walking back, past Marks & Spencer – they had a branch up in Fore Street then – and I saw a queue. I thought, 'What are they queuing for?' It was a consignment of Smarties that had come in! Sweets had just come off rationing, so I queued up and got some. I was lucky I had some money left…but can you imagine queuing for *Smarties*?!

We used to walk to Mount Wise open-air swimming pools; we'd go there weekends. 7 o'clock Saturday and Sunday mornings – right through from March to September. It was cold! Well, there used to be two pools – ladies and gents. It wasn't really segregated – the gents' one was just deeper and the men's changing rooms were by the men's pool and the ladies' by the ladies' pool. They had two pools there for a long time – now there's just one. It's free down there if you want a free swim. It was wonderful swimming down there. We'd be swimming along and we'd often see a Naval ship coming in, and it would look as if it was coming right into the pool! So summer holidays we'd be down there, or up on the Hoe in the Lido, but Mount Wise was shorter to walk from Stoke, so we tended to go there more than the Hoe, although I had a season ticket for both places, which was five shillings a year.

Maureen Baser

Image: Fotonow

Michael (John) Bridgewater, born February 1938, Devonport Maternity Hospital, Plymouth:

We were a very small, self-contained family. I have one sister two years younger than me. My father was an only child, and my mother was the middle one of three. Her older brother was away in the Navy until he was unfortunately killed in an explosion, in 1942. Her younger sister joined the WRNS as soon as she was able to leave home. My mother was married at the age of seventeen, and my father was a Lieutenant in the Engineering Branch of the Royal Navy. Initially my parents rented a house at the top of Milehouse Road, and then we moved in with my mother's parents in Stoke, after my father went away to sea. It was a large house – lots of big rooms, a big garden and we had live-in household staff looking after our household needs. My grandfather was a well-to-do businessman, he had a timber yard in Richmond Walk – down by the water – and a plumbers' supplies place, in Ebrington Street I think, but I wasn't conscious of social status at all, at the time. We were an old-fashioned, middle-class family, we knew right from wrong, did what we were told, dressed smartly, were polite to our elders, all the things you were expected to do in those days.

I was too young to recall anything significant but from what I've been told, when there was an air-raid warning, everyone would troop down to the garden, where there was a dug-out shelter that my grandfather had constructed and we were down there safe and sound when the house was being hit by incendiary bombs and the roof destroyed. I was told that my great-grandmother didn't like to go down to the shelter and would try to persuade my grandfather to let her stay in the house. Fortunately he was a strong-willed man, and the night the house was bombed she was with us down in the shelter. A short time after we left it was requisitioned by the Admiralty, and used for war purposes. My aunt tells lots of stories, she's still alive and ninety-two now, living in a care home outside Tavistock. She's actually recorded an interview for other purposes about her being a driver in Plymouth for the WRNS, and how she was terrified driving down Union Street with bombs falling down beside her, apparently.

We didn't leave the city because of the danger, but because the house was made uninhabitable and we had to find alternative accommodation, so we moved out to Dousland where we rented two properties near each other. My great-grandmother, my grandparents and my aunt lived in the small bungalow, and my mother, my sister and I and a friend of the family who was in the WRNS rented another house a few hundred yards down the road.

Our house was called *Edgemoor*, and it *was* on the edge of the moor; we would run on the moor, the old Princetown railway line wasn't far away so there would be occasional trains. There were ponies, sheep, cattle and adders sunning themselves on the railway line so we had to be a bit careful!

We were lucky that the bungalow where my grandparents lived had a yard out the back and they kept chickens, and the house we lived in had a garden and we were able to grow vegetables, so we had rather more fresh food than many people in the city.

My father was away continuously over three years so when he came home neither my sister nor I knew who this stranger was at the front door.

I remember coming into Plymouth on day-trips and seeing rows and rows of Nissen huts with stone fronts to disguise the fact that they were huts.

The Abercrombie Plan was a good idea at the time but, in retrospect, shortcomings didn't get noticed until it was too late. My major recollection is the wind howling down Armada Way, and no shelter from it! The rebuilding on the periphery of the city took a long time after 1945, although the main shopping area with Royal Parade, Dingles, Pophams, Spooners, the opening of St Andrew's Church and the restoration of the Guildhall were, quite rightly, sorted out fairly quickly as it was important for things to be seen as getting back to normal. But once you got out from the centre there were large gaps of bombed areas that were left for years and years and years. Houses where the ends had been blown off – I think there is one in Devonport where you can still see on the outside the fittings of the house that had been attached to it.

Where I live now, in Efford, it was all countryside then – farmland between the wars – and there was very little housing development up there. Then at the end of the war they built these massive new estates, so there were great big areas covered with prefabricated bungalows.

These prefabs were only supposed to last five years, as temporary measures to give people roofs over their heads, but they lasted much longer, even though some were almost like wooden cabins with flat roofs. People still talk about them now out there. But the Abercrombie plan catered for a lot of this redevelopment, and in its way it was brilliant, especially out at Efford, which is up on a hill on the edge of the city. Big, broad, tree-lined avenues were planned and dug, spacious semi-detached houses set back a little, with large rooms and a decent-sized garden behind, and unbelievable views over to Dartmoor and the Plym Estuary, and so on. It was almost like a marvellous New Town, right on the edge of Plymouth. And this was to be the 'New Age' for Plymouth! The only trouble was that in those days, they hadn't really catered for traffic, so there were no garages or provision for parking. But also this was the antidote to the pre-war overcrowding in the centre.

The first residents up in the Efford neighbourhood came from the very poor, overcrowded areas around the Barbican and the waterfront and they hardly knew themselves – they couldn't believe they were given so much space!

Michael Clarence Tristram Turpitt, born, and lives, in Oreston, Plymouth:

Well, I was born in 1937, in Rollis Park Road, and my earliest memory is when I was about two and a half, being bought into my grandparent's lounge and told to keep quiet, because there was an important announcement about to be broadcast on the Radio, by the BBC. It was the news that we were now at war.

In 1941, when I was four years old, the Germans scored a direct hit on the oil tanks at Turnchapel. My grandfather woke me up and carried me to the front window to see the flames and said, 'You will never see a sight like this again.' Up to seven firemen were killed there because the oil bubbled up over the tank and they were trapped. The black smoke billowed over our house for several days. On another occasion, the siren went and my mother picked me up and carried me to the back door to rush to the shelter in the garden. She stopped as we heard a 'rat-tat-tat' and we looked up and we could see a plane up above us which suddenly caught fire. It was a German plane and had been shot down by one of our ones. The pilot bailed out and was captured by farm workers at Tamerton Foliot. When told that he would be taken to Plymouth police station as a Prisoner of War he said, 'But there is no Plymouth, we've completely destroyed it!' or words to that effect.

Every night we would hear the Stuka dive-bombers diving and then the whine of their engines as they roared up again, you heard the 'whoomp' as the bomb hit...a bomb landed in a garden three houses away and left a big crater. In the mornings after a raid, we used to go out with a bucket and collect shrapnel and sometimes it was still hot! About six or seven incendiary bombs landed on the hard tennis courts opposite our house and burnt the tarmac. My grandfather picked up the bits of the burnt out bombs and re-tarmacked the surface. He had a gardener, an old deaf, mute man called Fletcher who used to dig a bit of the garden for his 'baccy'. Fletcher dug into the fin of an incendiary bomb and excitedly went to fetch my grandfather, who dug it up; it had landed on soft earth and not gone off. He put it in a bucket of water and when he thought it safe, unscrewed the bottom and poured the powder out. It stood on the mantelpiece for the rest of the war!

My dad, Arthur Douglas Turpitt, was a teacher at Devonport School, and the part of the school he taught in was completely destroyed so he was then appointed to help re-house people who had been bombed out of their homes and advise them where they could get meals. He was also in the Home Guard and would go off most nights to the rocket sites at the top of Staddon Heights – we always asked them if they'd hit any German planes, but they never did.

I remember, aged six or seven, going in with my grandfather to Barclays Bank, and whistling because I'd just learnt to whistle. He said, 'Shhh! You mustn't whistle in a bank!' So I never have! My mother was very Christian, and so we went to Sunday school in the morning, followed by a service in the chapel, then Sunday school again for the afternoon, and again in the evening we'd attend another service. Saturday night was bath night, and then we'd have clean clothes to go to church the next day. In those days clothes lasted a whole week. My brother was first in the bath, then my sister and I was always last – when the water was cold.

In January of 1944 there was a big raid in Oreston and a bomb landed on the air-raid shelter in Broad Park, eleven people were killed including two little girls from our Sunday school class. My father decided it was too dangerous to stay in Oreston and we moved to Chub Tor Road in Yelverton, the house of Plymouth historian, Crispin Gill, whose wife was a cousin to my mother. Crispin Gill was away in the war, as captain of a Royal Naval motor torpedo boat. My brother and I used to go to the Old Dame School in Yelverton, run by Miss Sammels, and one day two girls dared me to climb out of the window, which I did. They immediately called Miss Sammels and said, 'Michael's climbed out of the window, Miss!' No word that they had dared me! I denied it, and she threatened me with a six-foot curtain pole – to frighten me into not doing it again. I thought it unwise to trust girls after that!

When we moved to Buckland Monochorum we lived on a farm called 'New Farm' with Mr and Mrs Buckland and their daughter Jean. We went to the local Buckland school and stayed there until about 6th May 1945, when my dad came to collect us and said, 'The War's over!' May 8th the Germans surrendered and everybody in Oreston went mad, they had a big party in the Nissen huts where the barrage balloon was moored, they all got drunk and were singing rude songs. I went home and told my mother they had sung 'Roll me over...' She tut-tutted and told me not to go back there again.

Most houses had their ceilings cracked and windows were blown in, frames and all. They were all taped so they wouldn't shatter. Crews of men went around and fixed the windows on behalf of the Government for free.

One ceiling that I will never forget – it was early in the war and our class at Oreston Primary school, (for six year olds) Miss Groves was taking a class for singing, us boys could all sing because we all went to Sunday school, we were singing 'Heart of Oak are our Ships, Jolly Tars are our Men' and because we were singing loudly the girls started to laugh. One girl, Sylvia Brown, was laughing so much Miss Groves made her stand out the front and told her to behave. Miss Groves started playing again, and us boys sang even louder. Suddenly a big three-foot round piece of ceiling fell right on Sylvia Brown's head and she disappeared in a plume of white powder, and when the dust settled there was a distraught Sylvia Brown completely white! Miss Groves said, 'It's your own fault! If you hadn't been naughty you wouldn't have been standing there! We were crying with laughter – there wasn't a dry eye in the room!

Muriel Nora Marshall and her twin sister were born at 5, River Street, Truro, in 1921:

My parents were Victorians. Daddy was born in Liverpool in 1891 and Mother in Plymouth in 1896. We were working-class really, Granddad was the manager of an Avery Scales shop in River Street, Truro. Christmas was always lovely and he would bind coloured paper around a hoop. Also he used to pour brandy over the Christmas pudding and set a light to it, he was lovely, he had a little Austin Seven and we used to go to all the seaside places. We had very good manners; Mother wanted us to be bought up nicely. Granny's mother was an only child of quite wealthy parents but she eloped with the coachman – it was like Bleak House.

Favourite food...there was nothing that I didn't like particularly. My sister, though, didn't like going to guest houses and eating their food when she was on holiday, so we had to say that Granddad had sent it all from home, and I remember seeing green jelly wobbling on the plate and thinking, *Granddad never sent that!* Of course, Dad being in the Royal Navy he treated us like boys on the training ship – if we left our food he'd tell us, 'If you leave food on the training ship you'd have to eat your boots by the end of the week!' I had no other siblings, but was glad my sister and I weren't identical twins, I wouldn't like someone just like me coming towards me – must be a bit creepy! She had auburn hair.

We lived up in Liverpool, and moved to Plymouth when we were seventeen, and I worked as a hairdresser.

When we were both nearly twenty, we got called up, so we went nursing. We had wanted to join the Navy but Dad said, 'You're not going to wait on a lot of sailors!' So it was nursing, and you could choose what you wanted to do, so I went to the Civil Nursing Reserve. You didn't have to go along for interviews and things...they just took you on. We had training in Plymouth, but some went outside. I worked as a nurse at Greenbank but wasn't old enough to work with the injured because you had to be twenty, and I was only nineteen, so could only work with other casualties. We could have left after the war, but I wanted to stay there. I was at Greenbank Hospital and some wards didn't have a lift, so during the raids the patients who couldn't be moved would just have enamel bowls put over their heads!

Dad worked for Barclays Bank. It was top hat and tails in those days – the Bank of England wore red tails – and we lived on the top floor of the bank in Princess Square. It was called 'Barclays Chambers'. There was a big kitchen, two bedrooms, a dining room...before we got there you'd have a key to a little park, but it was later turned into a car-park, so there weren't gardens. We settled in lovely, and then on the 2nd March, 1941 the whole thing went up! Oh, it was terrifying! We were in the basement all the time during it. Dad was going upstairs to try and get some of the furniture down, but couldn't rescue anything. I was carrying two books, if anyone asked me what I saved from the Blitz it was, 'Two books!' I've hated the smell of burning since then; we had a Terrier dog as well...poor thing. You were afraid of getting buried, because you heard of people getting buried. We just sheltered in the basement, and then the wardens came and asked us to leave because it was all going up, and that's when we went to the church where we just wandered around until we saw an air-raid shelter – this was just after the bombing.

Mother had a big bag that she carried around, with insurance policies in it, and you could go to an office and they'd figure out everything you'd lost. If you lost a lot of clothes you got some vouchers. Mutley Plain was sort of all right. There was a shop called Wheelers there, and you could use your vouchers. On the night our home was destroyed, the wind was blowing strongly, and it was the incendiaries that did it; it was burnt down to nothing. People were wonderful and risked their lives to save others. There were communal feeding centres, and you could get a nice plate of food. Cafés were still open, but you'd get things like steamed fish because rations were on.

We left the city after the April Blitz, which got Devonport and the Dockyard. Even sailors in the barracks were killed. So for a bit of a break we went to Clearbrook and rented some rooms, but Mother didn't stay long. There was a farmer who accused our dog of worrying his sheep so she said she'd rather go back and face the bombs. She loved animals. When we came back from Clearbrook we went to Citadel Terrace, to a flat that was near the Hoe and near the town. There was a woman next door that Mother called 'Mrs Air Raid' and she would come into the shelter with us – the shelter was in the house. A lot of people had those garden ones, and used to sleep in them; I've never been in one of those.

After the war everything was gone in the city centre, but American prefabs had come over which could last about fourteen years, and people would excitedly say, 'They've got a fridge!' No one else had a fridge! And there was central heating...people loved them...they were all compact with all mod cons.

The rebuilding of Plymouth was an improvement. Before, by St Andrews church, you could smell exhaust fumes it was so crammed in. They had to do something. We could see the new plans. My mother and father loved it; I think it's much better now. It used to be so pokey. There were fish-carts and tiny shops...it was quite bad.

During the War there were dances on the Hoe and there were dances at the Continental Hotel that finished at half past ten. The cinema was there; they opened them up in the week when previously it was only weekends. I remember going to the cinema once with Grandma and Granddad and we were waiting in line and the usher came out and said, 'There's a Western showing and a drama, so hands up who wants the drama and who wants the Western?' so we all put up for the Western. You voted for what you wanted to see!

It was an interesting time. Like I said, I always had enough to eat, even through the war. I always had enough shelter; I had a little bit of money so I could live comfortably. I was fine.

Muriel Elizabeth Ellen Willis, born 1925, at Lee Mill, Ivybridge:

From the age of eleven to fourteen I went to school in Ivybridge and had to walk there from Lee Mill. It was about two and a half miles to Ivybridge, and then home. Leaving school at four o'clock and walking all that way it was a job to get home and get the kettle on by quarter past five – otherwise there'd be trouble! There were rumours of war of course. My father said to me one day, 'There's going to be a war,' but I knew that. I was quite intelligent; I knew what was going on. There was no point taking my 11-plus because if I'd passed we couldn't afford the uniform or books anyway, so I couldn't take the test. By this time my brother-in-law, George, was away on board ship and my eldest sister, who was married to him, had two children so she used to spend a lot of time with us, and I'd go into Plymouth and be company for her and the kids. War broke out on the 1st of September 1939 and I left school in August 1939 aged fourteen. I went to live with my sister and got a job. My first job was in an opticians; Leonard Gibsons, on Mutley Plain. I was nanny to his youngest daughter who was six months old – I enjoyed that. For my sister, I used to do all her shopping in the Co-op. The manager there said to go and work there, so I left the opticians and went to work in the Co-op, where I was measuring out the rations. Sugar was always in a blue bag, then two ounces of butter, meat I think was always on coupons. We got by – how I don't know. When war broke out everybody was flying for air-raid shelters and having gas masks fitted. You weren't allowed out anywhere without your gas mask over your shoulder. If they caught you without it you were in trouble. The lady that lived next door to us had twins and when I was on my half day, on Wednesdays, I used to take them out to Devil's Point in the pram. But one afternoon we got caught out in an air-raid and I didn't know what to do. The Air Raid Warden wouldn't let us go home, so we had to sit in the underground shelter there. Of course the poor mother of the twins didn't know where we were… but we got through that little bit all right.

I went to work in another Co-op in Chapel Street, which was a continuation of Durnford Street, really. You came down Durnford Street into Chapel Street and there was Plymouth Breweries. Before that was a pub called The Red Lion. Just up the road was a post office and that was demolished. Well, it didn't have a direct hit but it was damaged enough to kill it off. A cooked meat shop was down there, and she used to sell things like pigs trotters and chitterlings…it was a very popular shop, which was only damaged in the blast, but the chip shop opposite had a direct hit. Pubs closed at 11 o'clock, and the Marines always liked to stop at the chip shop and buy fish and chips on their way back to barracks. This night a raid was on, so they all crowded in the porch and as they were crowded…all clustered together…well…that's how they were found the next morning, all stood up dead in the chip shop doorway. You can't imagine that, can you? I couldn't work for a couple of days after that – we had to clear our shop out, and all the glass and everything had got in the food.

I used to travel by bus from the Harvest Home pub up where the University is, to work, and the raids were getting bigger and bigger. One Friday evening I got to the place where the bus normally terminates. There were lots of people there but no buses running. Because there was such a heavy raid on everybody had taken shelter but they didn't have Anderson shelters there, they had brick shelters – built against the wall – and everyone was crowded in these shelters. There was a terrific raid and I was afraid, but curious to know what was happening, so I stood in the doorway of this shelter and could watch the incendiary bombs falling, and as soon as they hit the floor they burst into flames, and *everywhere* you looked there were fires there. Of course they lit the sky up for the bigger bombs. The inspector for the buses came and said that there'd be no buses for the night because no one would take them out. I was stuck; I couldn't walk anywhere... At ten o'clock a driver came out and said if anyone wanted to go anywhere out of town, he was willing to try taking a bus and so we climbed in and he took us home. So I got back to my father's at Lee Mill, and at that time people were leaving Plymouth at nights on any vehicle they could; bicycles, lorries, buses cars, anything to get out of Plymouth, and they'd go in droves to get to the moors or any country place. After a few nights of this, the local vicar opened up the chapel in Lee Mill – which is still standing – as a rest centre. There were no beds, but anyone could come to this chapel, and they were lying on the floor, on the pews, everywhere and anywhere, just to get their heads down and get out of Plymouth. Every night. I used to go there each morning, I was only in my fifteenth year, but I used to get up at 5 o'clock and join a couple of elderly ladies, and we'd light the fires, boil the kettles and make cups of tea. One at a time, we'd wake them up and give them a cup of tea, so they could get to the Dockyard by 6 o'clock. I did this for three weeks. I said, 'From now on, I'm not going back into Plymouth again, while the war's on!' So I gave up my job in the Co-op and lived permanently with my father, taking a job on a farm, of all places, just outside Lee Mill, run by a family called Netting. They were ever so sweet, and I was young, and they had children of their own and so we all mingled in together, picking up potatoes, moving the hay around, looking after the pigs and the chickens. I did enjoy it.

We used to go out to Devils Point a lot, a gang of us. One with an accordion, one with a guitar, a whole gang of us, and the Air Raid Warden, as soon as the siren went, would make us go into the underground shelter. Several times out there I saw planes flying over the Sound, with blokes parachuting out. It was exiting because I was only fifteen and had never seen anything like it!

Everything was so austere during the War years. It was coupons for this, and coupons for that. You couldn't buy anything – and I was getting married! The lady who lived upstairs, at the time, took a pair of net curtains and made my wedding dress! She lent me a white ivory prayer-book which she decorated with lily of the valley and freesia. It was marvellous, I felt like a princess! Food was tight and we had cheese sandwiches at the wedding reception. A couple nights before the wedding, Derek and his dad went into every pub up through Union Street that was left from the bombing, but had to go right to the top to manage to get a couple of half pints...when he came home he had a bottle of wine that a landlord had given him, and that was the only drink we had for our wedding reception! Although after the war money was good, during the war it was very tight, everyone was poor. I met Michael Foot while I was canvassing the doors for election. He was a lovely man. So was Lady Astor – a lovely lady.

Muriel and Derek's wedding at St Paul's Church, Durnford Street.

My sister, who had four kids, applied to the Corporation and moved to a house in Derwent Avenue, Efford and in 1954, through the points system operating at the Corporation, I was allocated a house out at Austin Farm which had just been built and there was a huge garden, front and back – I had the two babies by then. We were one of the first tenants to move to that estate. There were no pavements or street-lights as yet. It was like walking through a muddy field all the time as it was still being built, but we coped all right. Instead of having an old tin bath, it had a bathroom! Instant hot water – just turn the tap on and there it was! No boiling up saucepans of water...it was fabulous, and my daughter had her own bedroom. There was a nice community, with a tenants association that organised parties, bingo, whist drives and what have you. My sister stayed at Efford until she died twelve years ago, she loved it there.

Derek was de-mobbed and worked as a window-dresser for Guinness for 34 years; he was posted to London. We all had to live there, and give up our Plymouth house and I hated it. I told him I was coming back to stay in Plymouth, so I rented a house in St Budeaux, which we had for five years, then we bought a house in Coypark Road, in Peverell, then to Sefton Avenue for a couple of years until we bought our house here at Leicester Close, where we've been for thirty-four years!

Muriel Willis

Image: Fotonow

Pamela Biscombe, born in Plymouth:

One day there was an air-raid on, and in those days we lived in a flat in Whiteford Terrace which had a large back garden with an Anderson shelter. Often when a raid started a lot of people would go under the stairs. What happened was there was banging on the door, I think Daddy was out in the back garden putting incendiaries out, I think he used to put sand on them. Someone went to the door and there was a very young ARP woman there and she said, 'Please come out! Your house is on fire!' In those days you always had some bags packed in case you were evacuated or something, so Mummy went to get her bag. Auntie, I think, was out for the night. We started down the steps and the ARP woman picked me up. I didn't want to cry, thinking it would look cowardly. But it had been so quiet in the house and suddenly the door had been opened and it was like a whole new world – so loud and the light was indescribable. There were search-lights everywhere and noisy anti-aircraft guns were firing, there was a lot of traffic – loads of taxis everywhere – there were chunks of glass around, ambulance sirens, bells ringing and fires... As we were going down the steps I think I may have said that I didn't like what was happening, or something like that, and the woman took off her tin hat and placed it over my head. I remember thinking, even at that young age, 'Oh! She's putting her life in danger to save me!' I will always remember that, and I can still feel, to this day, the feel of her warm, serge coat against my face. We eventually got down the steps and finally found a taxi that took us to my grandparent's house which was an Edwardian, two-storey house out at Derriford, which was in the country-side in those days. My dear old grandfather taught me to read before I went to school.

At the back of my grandparent's house there must have been a slope, or something, because the back of the house was terribly high, and there was a big garden with a large concrete patch in it. I was there with Daddy one day when all of a sudden, what should come into view…and you could see him as clearly as anything…an airplane with a big iron cross on it! It looked as though he was going to come into the garden, or knock the chimney pots off my grandparents' house! I can see that man even now… I think he was trying to lift the plane up – he must have been thinking, 'Oh! I'm going to hit this house!' Anyway, off he went and we never heard anything more of it, as there was no local radio in those days. Whether he was lost or crashed a few fields away, we never knew but it was an amazing thing to see.

One of my disappointments was that I'd been told by my parents that I'd get a Mickey Mouse mask, and a chap who had the job of fitting children with these masks came around – he looked terribly ill. I was very excited at the thought of this mask, but the man said I was just a bit too old – I shouted the place down in temper! Although Mummy asked if he could make an exception, he said no. They weren't used anyway. I went to St Dunstan's Abbey School, in North Road which was a convent school run by nuns. There were lay teachers as well and it had a nice atmosphere.

When I first went to school I went to Plymouth College Preparatory School; up from Mutley Plain. Margaret Smith, the headmistress, had supplied us all with tin hats for when there was an air-raid during the day. We used to have to run across the road to an air-raid shelter. She was lovely woman who always wore a blue-striped, or a pink-striped, blouse and she was the one who, after the Blitz that set St Andrew's Church on fire, went down there the next morning and nailed the '*Resurgam*' sign (I shall rise again) over what was remaining of the church door. It had been made with a hot poker and a piece of wood. It was there for years. Some years ago I took a group down to visit St Andrew's but it had gone. I wonder if it was thrown away... The air-raids were dreadful to come out to – everything would look like those photos you'd see of Berlin...everything was flattened.

Pamela Biscombe

Image: Fotonow

Pat Miller, née Aldersley, born 4th September, 1934. Lived in Hooe during the war:

World War Two broke out on September 3rd 1939, and that was the day before I turned five years old. So I started to go to school the day after war broke out, and my dad said the world would never be the same again. I think he was surely very right. I went to Hooe Primary School, and when the air-raid sound went, as it often did during the day, we would have to pick up our little chairs and go down into a trench that had been dug, and then sit in a single line in this trench. I was only five and didn't like this, as there was only one way in, no other way out, and I was afraid that if a bomb dropped near the school we'd be trapped, so I used to run home to my mum, only yards up the road at number 7, Westway. My friend Sheila Martin, who lived at number 11, Westway, she used to run home to her mum too, because our mothers always said, 'If we're going to die, then we'll die together.' Sheila and I lost touch but incredibly, sixty years later, I was at a local history conference and I re-met her! She now lives in Keyham – and we shared the story – we hadn't seen each other since those days! Now we're in weekly contact and have become, again, really good friends. You know the school never checked if we were there during the raids – they never knew that we both ran home. Once we were bombed in the playground – we could actually see the pilots aiming at us. Luckily they missed us.

My mother was a Quaker and they'd been helping the Jewish community in Germany escape to England. My father, who was a schoolteacher in the city, helped these young people find places to work on farms in and around Devon and Cornwall.

Interviewer: After the war did people's attitudes change?

I don't think so. People began to get their lives back together and the men came back from war, some were injured or mentally wounded. I don't think people realised about the mental problems that people suffered because of the sights and fear was real, but there wasn't much psychological help for those that came back. We used to go into Plymouth, and unfortunately some of the nice buildings that were left were knocked down to make way for this grid system, which we borrowed from Canberra, in Australia. It was disappointing to see buildings that were worth keeping being knocked down. There were no supermarkets then, we would get grocery items delivered from the farms or from the local shops in Hooe – there was a butcher's shop in the village. Go to Dean's Cross, maybe, for what we couldn't get in Hooe, go to Plympton to pay the rates, go to the electrical shop in Plymouth to pay the electric bill with cash; there weren't any credit cards!

I can remember the excitement when shops like Dingles first opened. My goodness me, we'd never seen anything like that, such as Armada Way, but it took a lot of time… There was an awful lot of rubble about for a long while, as a reminder of how things had been. There was still Westwell Gardens, with the corrugated huts that the Americans had used to live in; we eventually put shops there. Posh shops like Pophams moved up to Mutley and

Mannamead. Food rationing went on until 1955, and clothes were still rationed and in short supply because the factories had been geared up for making bombs and now had to ungear themselves to make clothes and boots and furniture…it all took time. Anyway people didn't have the money…you lived very simply in those days. You still shared what you had with your neighbours, you didn't have fitted carpets – you'd have a piece of carpet in the middle of the room and lino around the outside. There were no three-piece suites; you had a chair to sit in. No fridges or freezers, washing machines or dishwashers. You had a gas boiler, if you were lucky, so you had hot water and could wash dishes and clothes in the sink by hand. It was a *totally* different world.

I remember wondering how they'd ever get the 1943 'A Plan for Plymouth' sorted out. They didn't start building until 1946, and it seemed to be such a wonderful idea, but it made me wonder if it would ever come to fruition. There was such a lot of rubble to move first, and of course we weren't used to having all the men about to do all the work. Things were getting back to normal, but because I was five when war began, I didn't really know what normal was. War was traumatic for us – it was a lot to have gone through – getting bombed every day, living through a war… As little children we never talked about it, it was just part of every day life. We had the Japanese, the Germans and the Italians to contend with, and we had to do what we could, if we had to go short of food, have no petrol, no street lights…if that was what would help to win the war then that was what we had to do, and we were *glad* to do it and be part of it. We were very pleased to see the Queen when she visited on March 19th. As a little girl I was so proud of the Royal family – they meant a lot to us, very important. Yes, that was my biggest impression – of being *very* patriotic.

Interviewer: Did you have any celebrations after the war?

Yes we had a celebration for VE day and VJ day. All the families got together with trestle tables, flags and food but it was all a bit sparse because, to be honest, most people in the village were hard up, and until we'd beaten the Japanese there wasn't anything to celebrate. I mean, I had a cousin who was in the Army and had to go through the Burmese jungle and fight the Japanese. We felt there wasn't anything to celebrate until we'd won that part of the war. We were cautious of celebrating in case it all backfired and we found ourselves back in the war again. I remember that was a feeling that although we were free, it was a painful freedom, because so many people were lost so you didn't really have the heart to celebrate.

Interviewer: Did you have an overall feeling that Plymouth had improved because of the Abercrombie plan?

Yes, because the Abercrombie plan made sense out of all the chaos, there had been very narrow streets and buildings close together. Also housing estates were developed, and people got a semi-detached or detached house with a garden back and front, bathrooms, schools on each estate, a church, shops and a bus service to the city centre... That meant that people who'd been living in dreadful conditions in the city would be on the outskirts of it, with plenty of fresh air, and that would change their lives immensely. Their standards of living had been pretty awful. The authorities planned to knock down the Barbican! Fortunately a group got together to stop them doing that as that would have been a disaster. But the living conditions on the Barbican were horrendous, so yes, housing estates were built and that was a big plus, it wouldn't have happened otherwise. The airport was built and the ferry came to Plymouth. It originally came delivering cauliflower and broccoli, not passengers, but when it extended that bought trade into the city and meant that people passing through could get shopping – and that was quite something else for the city. The railway didn't alter very much. So after the war, I feel that people were happy to be able to sleep at night, there were more goods and food, people were coming back and there were jobs because industries began; Vi-Spring Beds came to Plymouth, Ford Cars were going to come, but didn't... There was a definite rise on the industrial estates with job opportunities for the men coming back from the war. The city became quite prosperous because the spin-off was there was more money to spend in the shops, and that was good. Much of the public transport closed down, but people began to get cars and motorbikes and that changed things a lot – bringing more industry – cars were mainly built in this country then. Plymouth city boundary changed, and Hooe became part of the city again, which was good. Yes, I think life improved in lots of ways in the city – we became happier and healthier. Without war I reckon Plymouth is one of the best places in the world to live.

Pat Miller

Image: Fotonow

Patricia Ruth West, born Greenbank Hospital, St Judes, Plymouth:

Interviewer: Where were you when you heard the declaration of war?

We had radio in those days, and we would turn it on, ears glued to it, particularly if Churchill was going to be on. He'd give us the courage to stand up to whatever happened. In the Girl Guides we'd have our parade the first Sunday of every month into the church, and sit in our pews – everybody was hoping there'd be no war, then the vicar came to give his address from the pulpit and said, 'I'm afraid I have some dreadful news for you all, Hitler has not responded to the 11 o'clock deadline, and we are now at war with Germany.' So it came over while I was at the church service.

The first twelve to eighteen months were termed the phoney war because nothing much happened. France fell in 1940, and our fear was invasion. Our beaches were closed and out of action and I was at Teignmouth with my father's sister and her husband, who ran a shop. Occasionally we'd stay with them. This particular time, when I was twelve, we had come down from the promenade to the very top end of the beach – we couldn't get onto the rest of it – and we suddenly heard a plane over the estuary and it started to lose height and then we heard, 'Rat-a-tat-a-tat!' and someone shouted, 'My God! Machine gun! Lie down! Lie flat!' There were about half a dozen of us, including my eight-year-old sister Rosemary. So we lay down and sand was shooting up everywhere from the bullets…luckily he was a bad marksman and didn't hit any of us, but that was very frightening. The plane then went out to sea, so we got up and dusted ourselves down and started going up the steps to the promenade when we heard another plane, and of course we were terrified by then, but when we looked around there was a Spitfire! He had gone out to sea – after this plane – shot it down and then come back. We could see the pilot, he made a gesture and then did the victory roll right over the beach. I experienced that. The following year I was going to be buried, and that was even more frightening…

Our house in Warleigh Road, Plymouth, just behind the Eye Infirmary, was built on a slope, so we had a cellar. We'd only just moved in on the Monday, and we were hit later that week. We weren't even on the street register there yet. The neighbours next door, who we hadn't had much of a chance to get to know over the few days other than, 'Hello!' and, 'Hope things are going ok?' shouted to my mother and asked if we'd like to share their Anderson shelter. Mother said that although she appreciated it, we would use our cellar. Why she said that I don't know, it's fate isn't it? The poor souls next door were all killed outright – blown to bits by a bomb. They were trying to bomb the railway line across from us. They dropped a land-mine that they used to set to detonate so far off the ground so that everything would blow out. Our house fell down on top of us. When we were in the cellar we used to sit on a wooden form and we would link ourselves together – my mother in the middle, my sister on the left with Tessa our cocker spaniel – they were inseparable

– and me on the right. And I remember this like it was yesterday – we were singing that old ditty 'Ten Green Bottles Hanging On The Wall' and we didn't even get down to 'Two Green Bottles Hanging On The Wall'... They managed to dig us out by following my mother's calls – we were lucky enough that an Army open van was passing by, looking to help soldiers who'd been hit and someone heard my mother's voice underneath the ground, shouting. They had to use their hands to dig for us – if they used a spade they could have hit us. They saw my mother's hand, and I was holding her foot although we'd been sat next to each other...my sister Rosemary, who was not quite ten, and our dog, were blown away from us. They got the full blast and were both killed.

* * *

Interviewer: Later, after the war, can you tell me if you were you happy or dissatisfied with the speed of the re-building?

It did take a while. They'd had Nissen huts opposite the museum where the University is now and they were used by the department stores to sell clothes; we had to have coupons for clothes. There was a lot of clearing up to do first, then all the planning of it – we were able to go in and see what was going on. We took it in our stride I suppose, after four or five years of upheaval with all that bombing, we were only too pleased that things were settling down and beginning to take shape. You can always find fault with the planning after, but then you think, 'Well, those that moan – could they have done any better?'

Pauline May Peak, née Rowe, born Norwich, 1923. Lived in Mildmay Street, Greenbank, Plymouth:

Pages from Pauline's notebook when she was working in the Plymouth Guildhall as an Operator for the Auxillary Service, as well as her day job as a secretary for Bond Pearce Solicitors.

The Guildhall was hit during the Blitz in 1941. She was 17.

March 20th

8.20 p.m.   practising Elocution
8.22 "   Mr McSkimming came & asked us to go
             to the R.C. as they were anticipating
             a spot of bother. (went down in two cars)
8.30 "   at the R.C.
8.40 Raid started & acted as Messenger & then
      receptionist.
12.50 Raid ended
                    Damage extensive
Daddy Stretcher bearing in the Hospital.
Mummy home all alone.
Ebrington Street direct hit from H.E.
29 Mildmay Street, only one pane out.

March 21st

8.15 p.m. set off for Report Centre
8.40 p.m. Raid started
8.45 p.m. Full Tenors manning the phones.
           Inc. Mr Simms being Relines.
           Irene Littlewood, Margaret & I were
           sent to the 13ᵗ Shelter.
8.50 p.m. Sent for to be Messenger.
           In the telephone room all night
12.4.5.   After the Guildhall had been hit
           Smoke came in, dreadful fire —
           had to abandon R.C.
1 a.m.   After walking down Old Town
           St. amid wreckage & through
           Market Avenue, passed Marks &
           Spencer's, & Costers, through York
           Street, all the time through
           blazing fires
           Caught special bus to Devonport
           They had a cup of tea all
           ready for us.
           Then lay on our beds until
           about 3 o'clock, after wandering

(R.C. = Report Centre)

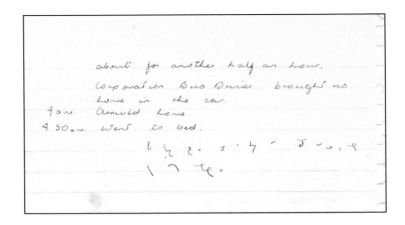

Interviewer: What are your memories of all the bombing?

I think the thing that struck me most was St Andrews church as a ruin, with the word *Resurgam* above the door... I can't even talk about it now as it makes me cry...It really hit me...but it did rise again, didn't it it? Bigger than ever now. So many people lost their lives...

Interviewer: But you did a very important job didn't you, in the basement of the Guildhall?

Yes. Well, we heard all the rumpus going on and the smoke started coming into where we were. These Naval dispatch riders came and guided us out and we made our way to the Devonport Guildhall, to continue where we left off in Plymouth. It was very exiting work that we did really, it sounded as if I was more a messenger than an operator but I did a lot of operating – getting first-aid parties, calling the fire brigade or the ambulance service if they were needed...it was a very exiting time.

March 20ᵗʰ 1941

8.20pm. Practicing elocution.

8.22pm. Mr McS…ing came & asked us to go to the R.C. as they were anticipating a spot of bother. Went down in his car.

8.30pm. At the R.C.

8.40pm. Raid started, I acted as messenger & then receptionist.

12.50am. Raid ended. Damage extensive.

Daddy stretcher-bearing in the hospital, Mummy home all alone.

Ebrington Street − direct hit from H.E. (high explosive bomb)

29 Mildmay Street − only one pane out. (Pauline's home nearby)

March 21ˢᵗ 1941

8.15pm. Set off for the Report Centre.

8.40pm. Raid started.

8.45pm. Full-timers manning the phones. Eric, Mr Sc..is, Edna Palmer, Irene Littlewood, Margaret & I were sent to the 1ˢᵗ shelter.

8.50pm. Sent for to be Messenger. In the telephone room all night.

12.45. After the Guildhall had been hit, smoke came in − dreadful fire, had to abandon R.C.

1am. After walking down Old Town Street amid wreckage, and through Market Avenue, passed Marks & Spencers, Costers, through York Street, all the time through blazing fires.

Caught special bus to Devonport (R.C.), they had a cup of tea all ready for us. Then lay on our beds until about 3 o'clock.

After wandering about for another half an hour, Corporation Bus Driver brought us home in the car.

4am. Arrived home.

4.30am. Went to bed.

Peter Edward Amey, born 3rd August 1935, in St Lawrence Street, & lived in Duke Street, Devonport.

Interviewer: Can you tell me about the food you ate as a child?

I had great respect for my nan. She was a right old battle-axe mind, but…great respect for her… She was short… used to wear an apron that crossed over at the back – the old fashioned one? Used to have a string through the sides and tied around the back. Hair up… She might do lunch on a Sunday, on an enamel bowl. The meat would go in the centre and all the potatoes on the outside. I don't know if you've come across sprinkling flour all over the top of the potatoes so they go crispy hard on top? Well, you know, it's just one of those things she did, and it was great and everybody loved it. I never liked cheese. What turned me off cheese was the fact you could only get one type…had that thick, horrible rind on it and it was just…*horrible*! And I never liked it until I went in the Army, and then I was so hungry…you had to eat it. Now you've got such a choice, haven't you? In those days you never had choice. Yes, and my mum was also an excellent cook. Excellent. Everybody said how good she was. Sunday was 'Sunday Roast', exactly on the dot of 1pm. You *had* to be there at one o'clock. While the dinner was cooking, she would make a sponge and maybe some little Eccles cakes…things like that. A treacle sponge with all desiccated coconut on the top – amazing Christmas puddings, chocolate log, pickles, jams…all that, my mum used to do. I can remember my first banana – because you never had bananas during the war. The NAAFI where

Mum used to work gave a christmas party every year for the staff and their children, and I can vividly remember going down there and looking at this yellow thing lying on the table and thinking, 'Well, that must be a banana!' It was a friendly neighbourhood and the one thing we all had in common was poverty, no-one had anything.

Interviewer: Do you remember what sort of values your parents instilled in you?

Lots of things really; simple things. My mother, she taught me how to say 'please' and 'thank you', always. 'Tie your shoelaces.' 'Count to ten'. Didn't matter what you had on – it had to be clean and tidy. To behave yourself, 'Don't be silly, or do silly things'! You represented your mother and your father. You remembered the family name and to keep their values, remember who you are. Especially when I was doing sport – I started wrestling at eighteen. Because you're not only representing yourself, you're representing your family *and* your country. So you've got to behave – not like these lunatics now! (Peter took part in the 1960 Olympics in Rome.) My mother was a stickler for discipline. If I did something wrong, she'd say, 'Right Mister! You're in for a week!' And I knew…I wouldn't be going out!

Do you know the Scott Memorial in Devonport, looking out over the estuary? When I was a kid, I couldn't have been very old and I think Dave Bacon (also interviewed) was there too. We were suddenly aware of these planes going in and out. I looked at him and said, 'What are they? What're they doing?' There were so many aeroplanes like you couldn't believe; we thought they might be from Mountbatten, across the way...they used to have big flying boats there. Used to land in the water and take off on the water... Anyway these planes kept on going in and of course *afterwards* we learnt that these were German planes – going to bomb Devonport Dockyard, and other places – bombing up in Plymouth and then coming out again. We actually *saw* them. We didn't know they were German because you couldn't make them out... Later on I said to Dad, 'Did you hear about those planes?' 'Where were you then?' he said. 'I was at Scott's statue,' I said. 'You silly little bugger!' he said. 'That was the German planes coming in to bomb the Dockyard and Plymouth!' I can remember that vividly! Things like that you know... There was a blind couple we lived next-door to...I think they were called Palmer...and they were down in the air-raid shelter, and they got up next morning and their house was gone...bombed. You know, that was our first contact with people that were homeless. I was young and thought, 'Well, where they gonna live?' you know? Just little things like that, that go through a kid's mind...and then it's gone because you're playing, or doing this or that... Next morning it was, 'What d'you get yesterday? D'you get anything? Shrapnel...?' Bits of shell, bits of this...bits of that...amazing really!

Interviewer: Where were you living at the end of the war?

In Duke Street with Mum and Dad...and my sister. Just the four of us.

Interviewer: And did you move to one of the new estates?

We moved to...well, they weren't new because they were built 1939 – a lot of the houses were built then – just before the war. At the time they were building the Ham Estate, and other places like that for people to move into because many blokes came back from the war and had no homes to return to – or the war damage repairs to their homes were not perfect but...done up enough to live in, you know? But with people like my dad, in particular, he'd never had a garden in his life, and so when they offered him this house in North Prospect, with a garden back and front, he just couldn't believe it, you know?

Where we had been I think was just three bedrooms – used to go upstairs and it was just bump, bump...the bathroom was downstairs. There was a coal bunker there, they used to tip coal in. You had to get coal...oh, that was another job kids had to do...get the coal in the scuttle to keep the fire going in the front room. Because you never had central heating in those days, and there was one fire and that was in the lounge. No TV. Radio – used to listen to the radio, especially the news, and if the news was on you're weren't allowed to talk.

Interviewer: Really?

No. Not allowed to talk while the news is on, 'Oi! News is on now. Quiet!' And that was it. You had to be quiet. I can remember that.

Peter Amey

Image: Fotonow

Peter Richard Tolley, born 1934, a nursing home in Greenbank, Plymouth:

Interviewer: And so when the Blitz began, can you tell me about your family and which house were you living in then?

My father, Percy Tolley, was a painter and decorator and he worked in HM Dockyard. He was a gifted man; he used to do sign writing. He was also an excellent helmsman – we were always sailing, and going to the beach in the boat, either to Bovisand or Mount Edgcumbe. My mother was called Gwendoline, who before becoming a housewife had worked in a hatchery, hatching eggs from chickens. Then there was my brother Graham, who is seven years younger than me. During the Blitz we lived at number 2, Albert View, in Stoke, and Albert View was between Pasley Street and Alcester Street, and it overlooked the railway – the main GWR railway – and shall I tell you a quick little story? The night this happened, in 1941, my mother was about three weeks off having my brother, so we decided to shelter under the bed during the air-raid. Dad, pregnant Mum and me. I remember hearing a stick of bombs, which were coming nearer, and nearer and my father saying, 'The next one's going to be close!' and so it was. The next morning when we looked out of the bedroom window we were right on the edge of a crater. What an incredible noise – it was very, very loud. Must have frightened my dad with my mother being so close to having her second child, and me still a child. I was frightened to an extent, I wasn't petrified but I was… yes…frightened. A funny thing – I don't know whether it's my memory playing tricks, but I think it is real – the kitchen was completely gone! The copper, into which you would put clothes – like a stone thing really – had had a thermos flask standing on it – and the thermos flask was still standing there – untouched! The kitchen gone, but this thermos flask still there, isn't that strange? We would normally have been in the air-raid shelter in the back yard, but on that occasion, because my mother was not exactly running around, we had decided to stay under the bed. We were then evacuated to Cornwall, to my mother's sister's house. My father returned to our home in Plymouth the following evening, and found that our house had been looted.

I went to the village school there in Pensilva, near Liskeard and stayed for about four years until the age of eleven, to do the scholarship. I do remember having to stay in hospital in Plymouth during that period at some stage. It was still during the war, and from Pensilva, which is on the edge of Caradon Moor, you could see the sky lit up in Plymouth. There would be air-raids, and my father and I would see flashes in the sky over Plymouth. When I was in hospital, Mum and Dad would be looking up at the flashes in the sky, and worrying, so Dad would come the following day to check that the hospital was still standing, before he went to the Dockyard to go to work. Seeing the hospital still there was great relief to him. Later he was given council accommodation as we had lost the house. After my O Levels at Devonport High School, and a brief period working in an accountant's office, I went on to do my National Service, in the RAF, in 1951.

Peter Tolley

Image: Fotonow

Ray Baggott, born 1938, in Swilly, Plymouth:

I was one of thirteen children and when the war started I was about three. My father, fifty years older than myself, was a short but very powerful man, and he dug us an air-raid shelter in the garden, which was the biggest in the area as there were so many of us. They weren't all home, three of them were fighting in the Forces, and others were working. He made such a good job of the shelter that the neighbours would come into our shelter when the bombs dropped as it was more secure than theirs!

After the war had ended, rationing went on for quite a while, and when sweets did come off ration we'd dive across the shop and grab whatever we liked – but generally we had no money anyway. When you bought a bottle of beer or lemonade, you put a penny deposit on the top of it, so the idea was to go around and collect as many lemonade bottles as you could. We used to salvage during and after the war, paper, rags and stuff like that. We'd collect it all up and put it in our home-made trolleys then push them all the way into town, to the bottom of Union Street and sell it all to Mr Knight – Knight & Nicholls that was – who'd give you a thruppence per hundredweight. You had to get a lot to go to the pictures – which was sixpence. Things were hard even after the war. There was a lack of clothing – me and my sister were the youngest, so we only had hand-me-downs or cut downs. My mother was a good tailoress – able to cut clothes down and so my brother's trousers would be cut down for me. You had one pair of shoes per year, so you had to look after them. When they got a hole in the bottom you'd put a bit of cardboard in to keep them going, you didn't know you were poor, because everyone in the district was the same, and we'd help each other out, one man would be working in each family and the mothers would stay at home and look after the children. They talk about poverty now, but it's different. *Everybody* was in the same boat.

The first school I went to was North Prospect. I screamed the place down when Mum first left me at the gates! I started school in 1943, when *most* of the bombing was over but we still had air-raids. One day we went to school and a big swan had been hit by the ack-ack guns and had landed on the roof. It was taken down and my friends had their photo taken, holding it up, for *The Herald*. If there was a raid during school-time there was a shelter in the middle of the playground and you all lined up and were marched off down there. There wasn't a lot of light, so you sat there and did mental arithmetic. Some of the teachers were very good story-tellers and would tell stories to keep us calm. Most shelters were four inches deep in water, so there were duck-boards to keep your feet dry. We weren't *really* frightened – being so young we didn't really know what was happening. The first house bombed that I saw was up the road, so we all went up to have a look, but then after that there were so many houses bombed you didn't take any notice. My sister had a little girl, and was bombed out twice, she had to be rescued twice and she went through a lot of trauma.

My father went to work in the Dockyard every day, came back for lunch, then went back again and they all worked hard. All the ships that were bought in damaged would be put in the harbour and they'd have to be repaired – rush them in, and rush them out – there wasn't much done mechanically then, things were done by hand. We had friends that lived on Normandy Hill, St Budeaux, and Mother would take us there once a week so we'd have to walk past the American camp. As we went by we'd ask the Americans for chewing gum or chocolate. (I *hated* chewing gum, never had it since!) They were very good to us, came around the schools and gave christmas parties. One party towards the end of 1943, when I was about five, just after I started school, was out at Roborough, and they took us there on lorries and we had a wonderful time. There were foods we'd never seen before – jellies, blancmanges, buns, cup cakes and chocolate, sweets... It was a real novelty to us. We came back with bags of them, you know. But myself, and six others from North Prospect School also came back with polio – there were two servicemen on the camp that had polio, and from serving us at the party they passed it to us. I spent the next two years in a plaster cast in Mount Gould Hospital and another hospital. First I caught what they thought was a cold...then chickenpox...and was put in the isolation unit at Scott Hospital, but it got so bad they said I'd got infantile paralysis, as it was then, and the priest came in to read the last rites as they didn't think I would last. They moved me to Mount Gould for about two and a half years and I was in a plaster cast from the waist down; my legs went completely. In hospital, if there was an air-raid, we'd been pulled from the ward beds, mattress and all, and put under the big table in the middle of the ward. That was frightening really, especially at night. Sometimes they'd take us out to the balcony, bed and all, to look out at the River Plym and see what was going on – it was very scary. In some ways it was an adventure because you could see all the searchlights and the planes going over... The nursing staff were very good at looking after all us children, everybody helped and cared for each other. Even all the neighbours cared for each other. If you asked me now I could name you most of the people from my house right the way up to Wolseley Road, as we were so intertwined. If anyone needed help others would come to their aid.

So, after the war we saw the old buildings being pulled down, and the new ones going up – we could see streets being made. Royal Parade was the first one, and the King and Queen came and opened that, and we thought that was great! Then we saw Dingles, Woolworths...and thought it was so marvelous seeing these big buildings being built. All the estates were built after the war around 1947, and here in Ham Woods, when the Army and Air Force moved out in '45 there was access to the woods, so we could go down there all day to play, and hide away. We thought it was really out in the country but in reality it was only half a mile away! We thought it was a big adventure to come to Ham Woods and Weston Mill to catch tadpoles in the big stream, and pick blackberries and pinch the apples from the orchard at the bottom. A lot of the houses around the city were rebuilt and people started coming back and buying them. But when Ernesettle was built no one wanted to live there! It was really out in the wilds then – out in the country! The city's grown, but I think it's for the best.

Ray Baggott

Image: Fotonow

Raymond Kilner Pashley, born 5th October, 1932 in Virginia Water, Surrey:

We'd moved from a flat in St Judes, to a flat in Elliot Street, on the Hoe, and we were there when war was declared on the Sunday. I remember my father saying, 'Right boy! We'll go down Tinside and have a swim, as it'll probably be the last one we can have!' So we went down and had a swim. My father had built an Anderson shelter in the back garden, it was semi-circular, with beds in it. I recall some years ago being up on the Hoe and there was a gate opened at the back of our old house and I could see that the shelter was still there! Definitely the same one. Father also supervised a lot of the public shelters going up in the area and many of the family ones. We slept in the shelter every night when the raids were on. Just me, Mother and Father – we had plenty of blankets, so it wasn't too bad really. When the bombing got very bad I was evacuated out to stay with my aunt, a very nice lady, in Yorkshire.

We'd get our rations from Blights, which was the food and stores shop down at Millbay, and Mrs Blight used to run it. Every Friday my mother, who came from Barnsley, made stew and dumplings, which I think was made to an original Yorkshire menu. I remember riding my bicycle along from Peverell to the Hyde Park area and there were tram-lines along the road. Halfway down the hill there was a horse and cart parked up with groceries. My wheels were stuck in the tram-line and I couldn't get out of them – so I crashed straight into this cart! I flew off my bike and went straight over the top and onto all the vegetables; I made a bit of a mess. I recall the railway line running from Millbay Docks, across the main road – just down from the Duke of Cornwall Hotel – and seeing these trains with all the troops on coming back from France, and we'd wave to them and they'd wave back to us – good fun that was. I recall seeing about forty thousand American troops at Slapton Sands. I saw them because my father had been supervising places for them to stay and making things okay, so landing craft could access the beach. At the end of the beach was a big house that, I think, was a hotel. He converted that into the headquarters for the Army generals to use as they were preparing for D-Day. The whole village of Slapton was evacuated so the American troops could be based there.

The sound of the bombs falling was horrific. The aircraft guns would be firing as well; there were several guns on the Hoe, and the Citadel had quite a few aircraft guns in it. There were big sea-planes at Mount Batten and others were moored by the Barbican, and they would fly off from there. Harrowbeer, at Yelverton, had really big planes landing there, and I recall a really big plane coming in to land at Yelverton that may have been a 'Flying Fortress'. We saw quite a few German planes when we were up on the Hoe, we were only a small country and how we were going to keep off this larger country...I didn't know. When you think of all the land he captured...we were lucky we had the Empire, but I still think it was the Americans coming in that helped us win the war. I was thirteen then and at Plymouth College. The atmosphere was very good, the feeling was *we stuffed the buggers!* There were street parties – it was all very nice.

Ray Pashley

Image: The Word Machine

Ron Henwood, born 9th October, 1928, in Devonport Hospital, Plymouth:

My earliest memory was in about 1931, the year my sister Joan was born and when I was about three years old. Mum and Dad ran a shop called 'Milican's', in Devonport selling pasties and pies. One day Mum, or maybe Dad, had lit the gas stove and put the match in an ashtray before leaving the room. There was a comb there with some hair on it that had caught fire. I picked up the comb to put the flame out, but the comb, being made of celluloid, stuck to my hand. The next thing I ran out in the backyard moaning and crying, and Mum shouted, 'If that's you teasing Joan, I'll come out and slap your bottom!' Then she saw me and almost fainted! Some children were evacuated but my mother always said, 'If we're going to die, I'd like us to die together.' So she kept us with her and we managed to survive the war.

We had an Anderson shelter built in the back-yard, which had bunks in it, and we went there every night and then if the sirens sounded we were already there. One night some incendiaries landed on our house and Dad thought it best to evacuate, so we went up to Charlie Coombes's Shelter which was up the road from Chapel Street, on an adjacent street called St Aubyn's Street, and off there was a little 'Ope' – you could drive your car down it – and there, down some stairs, was a basement that we called 'Charlie Coombes's Shelter'. Even leaving our house and running up to this shelter was dodgy, as the guns from the Dockyard were firing up at enemy airplanes and they were dropping bombs down on the Dockyard. You could here the bullets from the machine guns going, 'Bang-Bang-Bang...' I remember running behind my mother and my little sister Joan, who was then about eight. She was holding onto Mum's hand and I heard her crying out, 'Mummy! The glass is hurting my feet!' To which my mother replied, 'Shh! Be quiet or they might shoot you!' All hell was going on around us! Another evening – and fortunately my sister was away in Bovey Tracey for a fortnight with friends – my mum decided that she didn't think we were safe in the part of the public shelter we had been using, so she made us shift to a different section, and that later night the part of the shelter we had moved from took a direct hit. It killed the people who were sitting where we had been. We were breathing in thick, black dust – you couldn't see your hand in front of your face. For days afterwards we coughed up black phlegm – it had got right down into our lungs. We had to stay down there until the end of the raid, in all that dust, and then we had to climb up out through a grille, because the entrance had been completely destroyed and was closed off. We were so lucky. And *here* is the torch we used that night in the shelter – I still have it – you couldn't see three feet in front of you when we switched it on.

If the sirens went during the day when I was at school, Mum would run from her shop in Marlborough Street up the road to the public shelter in Morice Square. Mr Slee was the butcher, further up the road, and being deaf couldn't hear the sirens. If he saw 'Mrs Milican' as she was known, running up the road in her white jacket he would take it as a warning and go and shelter in his huge freezer. One day Mum was late, and a bomb landed killing Mr Slee who hadn't heard the warning. Mum felt awfully responsible about that for a long time, but if she hadn't been late, she may have been killed too. Us kids used to run around and play in Cumberland Gardens and Devonport Park and I used to go fishing down at Mutton Cove. I had a proper fishing rod while other children had bamboo sticks, but they seemed to catch more fish than I did! You had to fight your way to get to the rails to get your line down, at the pier at Mutton Cove where the swimming pools are – I'm not joking! Then the cry would go up, 'Mackerel up the wall!' and you'd see streams of mackerel chasing shoals of sprats along the wall, and then you'd start pulling up the fish. Most of the fish are gone now, and no-one fishing anymore, but catching fish was very handy what with the rationing.

In 1948 I was helping to build the new estates, I was a fourth year apprentice and working on the houses at Ham Estate. I also helped in the building of a school in Honicknowle, the Bush Radio Factory and was working on the flats in Union Street when I finished my training time in 1949. Ham Estate was all two and three-storey houses at that time. There was a lot of building going on, I remember doing war damage repair on properties on the Hoe, I worked and studied hard, and passed my City & Guilds in Carpentry and Joinery gaining more responsibility and respect from my boss Mr Simms, of A.N. Coles. In 1951 I was in charge of work at the Dingles shop, in Ivybridge in 1951 and my son was due to be born. The houses being built were lovely, with bathrooms

– compared to what people were used to, it was great! I remember the Abercrombie Plan, by then I was working as a junior building inspector. I was told that there were plans for three lanes of traffic to flow up Royal Parade but that the Ministry of Works would not fund that idea. Peyton-Watson, being a forward-looking man, also wanted three under-passes, one at the top of Royal Parade, one in the middle and one at the bottom. The Ministry of Works said they would not pay for under-passes, so he wasn't given the necessary permission.

William Henry Henwood outside his shop, Milican's,
14, Marlborough Street, Devonport.

Ron Henwood

Image: Fotonow

Ronald E. Jess, age 92, born in Plymouth. Lived in Radnor Place and Mount Gould:

The first night of the Blitz, I remember, was quite extraordinary. A friend of mine used to live down in the town, we'd go out quite a lot together swimming on the Hoe, and in winter times we'd go roller skating, and to the dance halls all around. He was very keen to own a motorbike and saw an Ariel Red Hunter bike advertised as up for sale at St Budeaux, near the Blue Monkey pub. This particular evening he called at my house and said he wanted to see what this bike was like, so we cycled out to St Budeaux, the bike was £33 I think – but he couldn't afford it. We set off for home but the sirens started and bombs were suddenly dropping all around. and there was a lot of glass on the ground and we both picked up punctures. So there we were, running along the road, pushing our bikes, and diving into various air-raid shelters trying to get home. It was quite heavy bombing but it didn't bother us although there was lots of shrapnel dropping down from the ack-ack. We ploughed on through it – from St Budeaux, along St Levans Road and up to Milehouse. He lived in town so we parted there and I then made my way across Central Park, eventually getting home – it had been quite a distance. First thing said to me was, 'Where *have* you *been*?!'

When I was eighteen I applied, again, to join the RAF – the recruiting office was in the Plymouth museum, in what's known as the Plymouth Room. I didn't say I was an apprentice this time, and was accepted and sent to Weston-super-Mare, where I volunteered for aircrew.

Once, we were on a low level bombing operation, the *Luftwaffe* was almost nil by then so it was all ground attacks. On this occasion it wasn't a very nice day and we were on order to attack a German HQ so we flew up there and we'd formed up to single file and were approaching the headquarters, I was close up behind number one in front, there was low cloud and I was fascinated at going down to this this target...and before I knew it there was great clatter right down through my fuselage it was like a lot of tin cans rolling around inside. I was hit quite a bit with ground-fire and damaged my rudder. I was thrown over onto my back then pulled away from the flack. I jettisoned the bombs and looked for a place to land. The chap behind me told me to climb, so I gained height and was all on my own, the instruments were toppled. I saw the sun and knew I had to go back south-west. I contacted ground control and they told me to fly ten degrees to the sun. I had great difficulty flying back, having to do a lot of manoeuvres, and when I got over Arnhem, the petrol finished so I started to come down. There was a river – Germans were one side, British the other – I managed to get across the river and I spotted a lovely field that I wanted to get into, and as I got closer there was a farmer there still ploughing the field. He looked up, saw me, then ran! I pulled up and managed to land on the other side of a row of poplars, I was knocked out temporarily; I'd landed on an ammunition dump! I coped with it and had a medical but was alright, grounded for a week then hitched my way home for a few days. I was one of four hit that day, one was killed, two captured but they escaped, so I was fortunate really.

Ron Jess

Image: Fotonow

Ruth Hocking, née Dawe, born in Plymouth, and evacuated with her family to Bere Alston.

Interviewer: Where were you born?

At Stoke, in Plymouth, shortly before the outbreak of the Second World War.

Interviewer: How long did you stay in Stoke for – were you there throughout the war?

We were evacuated around '40/'41 to Bere Alston as a family, and we stayed in a house at the top of Bere Alston for a very short while, then moved down into the village where we had a little rented cottage and we were in that until '46/'47.

Interviewer: Was it normal for a whole family to be evacuated like that?

Yes it was. Our parents wouldn't be separated from us, it was all or none! I have no idea if my parents organised the accommodation.

Before we were evacuated my dad would put us all in his little Morris car in the evenings and take us out to Clearbrook for safety purposes, where there wasn't any bombing. All five of us would sleep there in the car, and then he'd bring us home in the morning and go off to do a day's work. Lots of people would leave Plymouth in the evening to return the next day; we got to know so many people out there. I'd run around chasing a ball – I expect the boys would play football. My dad wouldn't have the family broken up – he'd say, 'It's all of us, or nothing.'

Interviewer: Was there much fear?

I was so well protected I never knew fear – I don't remember it. If we saw or heard planes, my parents made so light of it that it didn't frighten us at all.

I had a cousin just a few months older than me, who lived out at Derriford – where the hospital is now. Then there was a large fifty-bedroomed house there and her parents were the housekeepers for it. It had a very long drive with all Army huts down one side. We'd spend alternate weekends together, weather permitting. Sometimes we'd go up on the Hoe – swimming out to the rafts, or under the fountains, and when she came to me we'd be on the beach where my father had made – or somehow got us – a ten-foot dinghy, and it was such fun – ten or twelve of us in it sometimes, and occasionally it would sink and we'd have to wait for the tide to go out to be able to retrieve it! Then we'd pull it, with its oars and rowlocks, up to the corner of the beach and leave it there and no one would touch it until we went back there again.

Interviewer: Was there much awareness of the war out in Bere Alston?

Yes there was. My brother remembers a plane crashing in Grantham woods, and four or five people were killed – they were buried there where it crashed. He cycled from Bere Alston to the woods and saw them taking bodies from the plane. I think they've been removed now. It's recorded in the book *Plymouth at War*.

The only form of transport was the train, and I took my

husband back there years later to let him see where I was. We drove from our old house down to the station, and he couldn't believe that at that age we had to walk so far and thought nothing of it! I was only a little toddler. My father had a piece of land at Wembury, with an old-fashioned tent up there and he and my brother would go up once a month in his little car, for a weekend – they were only allowed petrol once a month. When I came along he needed more than a tent, so he built us a little wooden holiday home.

When we were in Bere Alston, after getting bombed out of Stoke, we couldn't find anywhere to live, so he said, 'I'll build my own home!' He applied for a licence and he was told he'd have to be part of a circle of 'self-builds'. I think there were six in that circle, if you were an electrician or a carpenter or a plasterer, say, you all moved around and helped each other, but then your own place tended to get left behind because you couldn't get on and do what you wanted to do, so it took several years to build them. I think they started in '41 or '42 – digging the foundations – but we didn't actually move in until '47 or '48. Materials were very difficult to get, you could only buy stuff that had been Blitzed and bombed – recycled materials. You'd buy a lorry load of bricks and they'd be delivered up to Wembury with all the cement and cladding, or whatever had been on them, and then Mum and I would have to clean them up! Our target was fifty bricks a day – chipping all that off the bricks with a chopper so that my father and brother could lay them that evening when they came home from work or school. I'd carry blocks, and slates if I could, I'd get the water, two or three times a day, in two cans – I couldn't carry much as it was quite far away. There weren't cement mixers then, so I also helped to help mix the cement up.

Interviewer: How did you regard that sort of chore?

Loved it! My parents were so good to me. I had such a very happy childhood and as long as I was with my dad I didn't care what I was doing. When it was being built, we'd go up there in the summer, and I'd change schools moving back to Bere Alston in the winter. Dad bought two single-decker buses and joined them together, end to end and *this* plan shows that the total space was fifty feet long and about eight-feet wide and we lived there, at Wembury, while the bungalow was being built. The bedroom was at the back, he raised the beds very high, with steps to get up them, and all our belongings – clothes and shoes – were kept under the beds in boxes; he was quite ingenious to do this. If you remember the old buses – the seats went down the sides – so he took some of them out and made a table to go in the middle, we had a settee and chairs, we even had people come up and stay! The driver's compartment was turned into the kitchen. We had to fetch water from a long, long way away, but we had a folding sink that they use on boats, he'd bought one of those cheap somewhere, and Mum used to cook on a primus stove – she had two – and a Rippendale cooker. My dad built a toilet at the back of the garden and he even put a trellis going up. He had time for everybody, and if you wanted a favour he would do it for you, he seemed to know every body.

Sheila Pauline Margaret Allen, born 1933, in Devonport Maternity Home:

Dad worked in Henry Lowrey's – a builders merchants. He worked in the shop most of the time. Mum was a married lady and they rarely did outside work in those days, so she was a housewife all the time. Her name was Vera, Dad's name was Harry. We lived in Peverell Park Road, with a little garden. Mum, Dad and I lived in the top flat and Mum's parents lived in the downstairs flat, but most of my memory of that time is that we lived all together as one family. I had four adults telling me what to do. I was very well looked after because of that – I had to do what I was told, but I guess I'd have to say perhaps I was spoilt a little bit!

It was the neighbours who had an air-raid shelter built – Grandad really didn't want one. The neighbours said, 'Share ours' and between them they took down part of our dividing wall in the back, just enough concrete blocks for us to get through the wall, so when the siren went we just had to run up a few steps, go through a hole and join our neighbours in their shelter which was very nice for us.

A bomb landed on our house the night Plymouth was virtually destroyed. As we lived upstairs it went straight into Mum's china cupboard and smashed all her china – she was so upset. Luckily it didn't explode. Obviously we heard it – we didn't have an air-raid shelter then so we were in a cupboard under the stairs. Mum grabbed Gran and I. Being a very careful chap, Grandad always kept a pair of long fire tongs with him – he had these in his hands at the time and he dashed upstairs and after opening a few doors and cupboards eventually found the unexploded bomb. He grabbed it with the tongs, took it downstairs, out the front door, down the steps, crossed the road, and tossed it into what was then just a field opposite, next to Venn Lane. He came back to the cupboard, where we all spent so many evenings – and told us he'd tossed the bomb into the field and that was that! There was not much space under the stairs – there was a bench with just room for the three of us to sit there. Grandad wouldn't come in – he'd stay roaming around the house ready with his tongs to do anything needed – if another bomb came in he'd pick it up and throw it out. We were very fortunate, *and* he managed to keep his garage business at Milehouse open throughout the war – he wouldn't leave Plymouth. When I was five or six my sole aim in life was to work in Grandad Pengelly's garage and to be able to sell petrol!

My dad was away in the RAF, and after we left for the safety of Minehead to stay with my uncle and aunt, my grandad, along with a group of friends, would go out on the moors every evening, for safety. He'd never learned to drive, which I always thought was odd for a garage owner, so he went with these men and they camped out there every night, as there was no bombing on Dartmoor.

I think we were incredibly lucky that the only bomb that landed on our house threatening us came when Grandad was there to deal with it.

Margaret Allen

Image: Fotonow

Sheila Soroka, née Martin, born 1935, Beacon Park. Moved to Hooe, aged five:

I was only four when the war started. I think one of my earliest memories about the war was being on a bus coming home with my mother, Dorothy, and we were opposite North Road Station and the siren went. Immediately a plane seemed to be directly overhead. The conductor didn't want us all to get off the bus but someone insisted that we get off. There were some big houses up a bank, and the owners very kindly opened their doors, and said we could go and shelter in there. Of course there was one mad scramble to get up all these steps and my mother managed to fall and let go of my hand. I got swept up the steps with everyone else, and I can remember just standing around in that hall looking around…and there was nobody I knew. Then I heard my mother's voice calling, 'Where's my baby? Where's my baby?' We eventually caught up together, but she was in an awful state – she'd cut knees and lost her hat – it was a big thing in those days not to have your hat…and that is my earliest memory. As a child it was frightening not knowing exactly what was happening and knowing that I was somewhere on my own – without my mother.

When we lived in the bungalow we didn't have an air-raid shelter so we used the one our neighbours had. There were about six bungalows in a row and four of us used that one shelter. Sometimes it was quite fun to sit up at night and listen to the grown-ups talking – you don't realise the seriousness of it when you're young. I remember my mum telling me to put my head in her lap and try to sleep. The noise was quite bad, on one occasion I was sure I could hear the whizz of a bomb and next minute thinking, 'Oh! I can't breathe, what is it?' They all thought the shelter was going to be hit and my mother had put me on the floor and was lying on top of me to protect me. I struggled and then suddenly I could move and thought, 'This is lovely!' then we all sat back up and it was all back to normal! It's more worrying and frightening looking back on it that it probably was to us, as children.

I went to junior school in Hooe, which was very small, there were only five classrooms in the corridor. I was there until I was eleven when I took my scholarship and then went to Plympton Grammar, leaving when I was nearly seventeen. I always liked English – writing stories – and I remember we had air-raid shelters across the field dug into the earth, which were horrible smelly things when you got in there. I remember the sirens going and trying to run home, because the shelters were not nice. Every now and then they'd come and test your gas masks, they'd take you into this van-like thing and the gas was there – when you came out they'd examine you to make sure your eyes weren't watering. I enjoyed school very much.

Another thing I remember – we were living at Beacon Park then and we'd have the wireless on and we heard that Devonport had been very badly hit. My mum's people came from there she was obviously very worried. She said that when we'd had our breakfast, we'd go and make sure Grandad was all right. So we got on the bus at Beacon Park and got partway through Keyham, but the road had been bombed so we had to get out and walk, and I can still smell it now, the burning stuff from all the fires, and all the rubble – an awful earthy stale smell – and being turned back by wardens who were telling us to go another way. When we finally got round to where my grandad was living there were lots of people standing around and we discovered that an unexploded bomb had landed at back from their house and Grandad was in an awful state because he kept all his money in a cashbox, hidden in the coalhouse. He managed to dive underneath a police-man's arm to go and scrabble around in the coalhouse to get it! He found it and came running out with it saying that there was no way he was just going to just leave it there. Smells are very provocative and linger on in the mind. They couldn't go back into the house until it was sorted out, so they all came to us at Beacon Park, but when we arrived we found our gas and electric had been turned off and so out in the garden we used metal buckets for cooking – they had holes in them and were filled with coal. So there we were – cooking in these buckets out in the garden. As children we thought it was fine fun! We didn't realise the seriousness of it.

My uncle, who worked at Mount Batten, had this really scruffy dog called Tiger that used to go with him to work. Tiger would also follow anyone else wearing an RAF uniform. Sometimes he'd be gone a couple of days – up in Mount Batten. One day an airman that my uncle knew had gone to Friary Station, in Plymouth, to try and catch the last train home but just as he got there the train was pulling out. Then Tiger appeared – racing up the platform towards him! The airman then thought if he hurried he might be able to get the ferry over, on the Barbican, so he went haring off and when he arrived – there was Tiger waiting for him, panting like anything! The airmen often took him with them, so I suppose he just knew his way around. He was a very intelligent and happy dog but sometimes it took ages trying to clean him up. He would often be covered in oil from spending time with the men on the boats. There were so many stray dogs on camp that they'd have to be shot, but not Tiger, he even had a pass – everybody knew him.

I can remember going into town when we were young, and literally there were nothing but bomb sites. There was a little Pannier market with stalls on it. Most of the big shops moved up to Mutley Plain, the town was just a mass of bombed out buildings. The children's ware for Popham's was in a house in Charlton House, up from Mutley Plain – and it was quite a jump to get from Hooe to there for school uniforms and things. We knew that 'Old Plymouth' was going to be rebuilt – we'd seen the plans and we'd think, 'I don't know how they're going to do that – it's never going to work!' I think Dingles on Royal Parade was the first, and I remember everyone wanted to go there to see it. It was a fantastic big store right in the centre...wonderful, but now looking at it, it's all old hat, the buildings we thought were so wonderful – they're thinking of pulling down! The plan was to have a straight road from North Road Station to the Hoe, and people thought that was ridiculous, but when you look now it is there - so not as far-fetched as it seemed. It was really quite alien to older people – they tended not to like it.

Sheila Soroka

Image: Fotonow

Sylvia Berry, born 1931, Prospect Row, Devonport, Plymouth:

I can go back to the age of 3, when we used to go to school in the afternoon, St Stephen's School, that's when we moved to Clarence Street. We were just ordinary working class people and lived in a corner house, shared it with three other families, then the pub, couple of houses then it was a school, and my mother used to put us in there afternoons and you'd go to sleep on a little camp bed – that's how we started off, all of us!

We were a happy home, we had to do chores as children and do the errands for our mother, and when we were on summer holidays my mother would take us to Central Park, to walk, or we would go across in a little boat at Mutton Cove and go to Cremyll, and then we would pick winkles off the rocks, and my mother would come home and cook them.

I never saw much of my dad, he was a Navy man and he was always away. My mum was a wonderful mother, very strict but wonderful and she loved us all dearly. I had two brothers and five sisters. Families were scattered in those days, but we always got together when my dad was home, but we just had a basic childhood where we went to school, and had holidays and we went to Mount Wise. My mother used to say, 'Right, you older ones look after the smaller ones down at Mount Wise!' Then when the war came we were all together when the raids used to come and we'd run to the shelters. My mother had Doreen, the baby, under her arm, running…we used to go down to Mutton Cove where they had the underground shelters and we'd go in them. You came out in the morning and you didn't know what you were going to face; people crying, houses bombed, picking up belongings...we used to run round the corner to see if our house was still standing and we were lucky that it was. Then we'd go round and pick up shrapnel – the Air Raid Wardens used to give us kids a shilling for it. Where we lived then at 45, Clarence Street, we only had back courts – that's why we used to go to the public underground shelters. At first we used to run to the shelters near the flats but then they put underground shelters down by the Dockyard wall, and on top of that, on the opposite side, they had an anti-aircraft gun, and they used to fire from there, it was tremendous.

A lot of people never had homes left, one friend of mine got killed – a family in the next shelter to us. We had windows blown out, things smashed, but touch wood we weren't too bad. Then when it got very bad – when we had the big Blitz – well that was terrible. The authorities would put us all in a lorry and take us out to Ivybridge for the night. They'd lay us on little beds in the church hall until the raids were all over – it was wicked – I mean every night, running and crying... Even when you were at school you'd hear the air-raid sound and you'd have to run home from school.

We were running home one day and because we lived near the Dockyard there were planes above us firing – and they were firing at us! I will always remember it. We just got inside the door when the guns hit the side of

our house. Nothing but bullet holes across the house...
I mean, I talk about it...my other sisters can't remember
that...but I can, and it was hectic. I used to think of my
mother every night taking us kids down to the shelter, but
my oldest sister wouldn't go – she said to my mother, 'If
I am going to die, I will die in my house' so she used to
stay there. But there you are, you see we were lucky, we
survived – they were frightening years, I tell you, I never
thought we would get through it, but we did.

In 1945 my mother got a notification when they built
North Corner, which is Cornwall Street, and they offered
her a large flat which we all grew up in and got married
from. It was the first time we ever had a bathroom; it
was so strange! Before we used to have a tin bath, and
she would bring it up from the back yard twice a week.
Wednesdays and Sundays we used to have our baths,
and then she would have to take all that downstairs and
empty it. Everything, including running water, was downstairs in the back yard. She used to have a two-gallon can
and she'd use that to fill it up. Out on the landing we
used to have an old-fashioned wash stand with a big basin
and jug to match so that all of us kids could have a strip
washes.

Sylvia Berry

Image: Fotonow

Ted (Edward) Jones, born 1934 at 15, Wyndham Square, Plymouth:

Interviewer: And what is your earliest memory?

I was six and a half when I had this experience. On this particular night I was sitting in an air-aid shelter at Wyndham Square during a bombing raid by the Germans, when an incendiary bomb landed at the back of our shelter. Minutes later an Air Raid Warden told us all to leave the shelter and go to another one in Wolsden Street. This was a terrifying experience for all of us because clusters of small incendiary bombs were dropping from the sky as we dodged from one doorway to the next, to get to the next shelter. There was a continual shattering of glass as the bombs went off. Approximately ten minutes after leaving that shelter we were told the house we'd been living in had been bombed, and that we'd have to wait in Wyndham Square until after the air-raid and alternative arrangements for our safety could be made. We all ended up at a community hall called the 'Wyndham' at Devonport. We stayed there for several days then moved to another community hall in Plympton. During that same evening the hall we'd been staying at previously was hit by a bomb. For two or three months we stayed until the Plymouth Council settled us in a house in St Budeaux, the rent for that house at the time was one pound, twelve shillings and sixpence a week – but we didn't have to pay. Moving from one community hall to another, it was community in that we just slept alongside each other, fed and watered all the time.

Interviewer: How often did you go into the centre of Plymouth?

Regularly. Once, sometimes twice a week, both socially and shopping, we used to go to all the cinemas that were there, you'd take your dinner with you and queue up at dinner-time at the Gaumont cinema, then go in and sit down to be entertained by the bloke who used to be on the organ, then have your lunch, see the first film, then would come the second half – a bit of singing would go on sometimes. There were A and B pictures, A was the main picture – you'd pay about 3s 6d for that, that's about 17 and a half pence in today's money! There used to be a big building called the 'Harvest Home' and down the side was a big espresso bar which used to be the meeting place for all the youngsters before you'd go on a night out. I used to go dancing in the 'Park Ballroom' and that sort of thing. Social life in the evenings was wonderful; there was no fear of getting mugged, you could just enjoy yourself. It was good.

I remember that buses during the Blitz would take Plymouth people out onto the moors when the sirens started, and the large area in the Plymouth Argyle football ground would be used to store some of the more expensive furniture and belongings – but even that got bombed and burned down. During the Blitz a small incendiary bomb landed in our attic when we were sheltering in our Anderson hut in the back garden at 8, Brockley Road, Laira, but it was soon sorted out by the Air Raid Wardens, who were there at the time.

We made sure we took something to the shelter to eat, and a flask of coffee, and we'd play cards to amuse ourselves and try to forget what was going on outside. We all *knew* that no matter who we were, how young or old we were, that if a bomb hit us, we were going up. There was just an acceptance that you could be killed, and I think that took away a large percent of the fear.

The next street over from us had a big quarry at the top of it and it had two attack guns there and search lights. It was quite exciting for my brother and I, being in the Anderson shelter, because when an attack was taking place we would pop our heads out from our shelter and watch the guns firing up and the search-lights criss-crossing across the skies, although we never saw the guns hit any aircraft. We felt that there was no fear there of getting hit because they were the next street over – you could see the ack-ack guns going like hell, and the search lights all over...mind we got told off by our father and had our ears boxed for doing it, but we just couldn't resist the temptation! That perhaps was the exciting bit of the war, although it was dangerous.

In Plymouth there were two big community air-raid shelters that were bombed, one was in Portland Square and that took a direct hit – all the people died there. The second community shelter bombed was situated at the bottom of Lydford Park Road, Peverell just at the beginning of Central Park – where my wife used to live. This was a much worse situation, the shelter was hit several times and many neighbouring families were buried alive. Bore holes were drilled down, through the concrete, to enable community members on the outside to speak to those who were still living and several attempts over the next few days were made to rescue them, but unfortunately the whole shelter collapsed and those that were still alive down there died.

In 1952, just before I went in the Army, the council moved my parents and me to a nice two-bedroomed house near Eggbuckland Road in Efford. It was in a cul-de-sac of about six or seven houses and everyone knew one another and helped one another. During the war in our previous home we'd had no bathroom. You'd have a bath once a week, in a long galvanised tub that Dad would fill with water, and we'd all take turns. Sometimes you'd come out dirtier than when you went in! The toilet was outside in the back and we never knew what toilet roll was, we just had squares of newspaper pinned to the wall on a nail. Our new house had a huge back garden – so big that we grew every type of vegetable there was. We grew so much we gave it away to our neighbours because there was too much for us to eat. The community stayed together for many years...we knew all the names of our neighbours. Back then, because we all knew one another, if somebody died in the street a collection would be made. Here, for instance, we've had three deaths recently and no-one ever knew who they were... That's one difference between those days and today. I thought the Abercrombie town plan was all right; a bit rigid – you couldn't get lost – there were only three streets to go up and down. It was a bit regimental, I would say. But it was probably the best financial way of doing it.

Ted Jones

Image: Fotonow

Tom Savery, born in Lipson, Plymouth, lived in Hooe during the Blitz. Former Lord Mayor of Plymouth:

My very first memory was standing with my mother in Woolworth's and she was saying how sad it was about the King dying. This would be January 1936. I remember also that there was the two minutes silence when everyone stopped in the street. The 11th hour, of the 11th day, of the 11th year celebrating the end of the First World War. I remember everyone…and buses…stopping, and men doffed their caps and everyone stood still in dead silence for two minutes. I remember that vividly – I was two or three.

For about three years during the war virtually the whole of the village of Hooe, where we lived, slept in a tunnel, would you believe? In those days Hooe was just a small village outside of Plymouth. At lower Hooe, in those days, behind the Old Vic (The Victoria) pub, there was a disused quarry belonging to FJ Moores, and there was a tunnel driven through from that underneath the lime-stone of the quarry right through to Hooe Lake. It was about three or four hundred yards long and about as large as the channel tunnel, probably, and for at least three years, everyone from the village slept there. Every night we would all take down our sleeping bags and then we would leave about 7 or 8 o'clock in the morning and go home and have breakfast… Over the course of time the walls of this shelter were cemented, they put in toilets and electric lights, and they built blast walls. We did that until the bombing stopped…

I was the child of a second marriage, and my father, who was in the Royal Navy and had fought in the Battle of Jutland, was fifty-years old when I was born. One day he said to me, 'Look, Tommy, you've got to be a brave boy. Your friend Jimmy has died.' Jimmy – I think he was called Robertson – I'm not too sure. What had happened was that he and his parents and siblings had taken shelter in their house in Hooe underneath the stairs. The house had received a direct hit and flattened it. They were un-injured, but they were trapped in the cupboard and the gas main fractured and they were all gassed. He had to lay them out... I remember at Hooe School seeing on his desk a vase with a white chrysanthemum in it.

Coventry gets the mention because that was the first one Blitzed in 1940, and the centre of the arms industry, but Plymouth actually was the worst damaged city in the whole of the country.

I remember the American soldiers, of course. They took over when they came over. I remember just before D-Day, the Sound was absolutely jam-packed with craft. You could almost walk from Jennicliff to Mount Edgcumbe on the boats, you know? Absolutely jam-packed and after D-Day I went up there with my parents and it was empty. Everything had gone. All the craft had gone. So yes, I remember that.

I remember hearing about the Abercrombie Plan on the radio when it was announced – I was doing a jigsaw on the floor or something – that a new plan for Plymouth was planned. I remember that vividly. And Abercrombie, actually, was a consultant. The brains behind it were Paton-Watson's. And before the war, I dimly remember that it was very hard to get to the Hoe because the whole town was such a higgledy-piggledy mess. You couldn't find out how to get up to the Hoe! Someone realised that the centre of Plymouth is saucer-shaped and that Derry's Cross is actually below sea-level. In 1959, because there were high seas and heavy rain, there were floods, and Derry's Roundabout was suddenly under water – sea-water – it had come back down through the storm drainage system. This demonstrated that Derry's Cross was below sea level. Anyway, the planners had the idea of sweeping away the confusing town layout, so that when people arrived at the railway station they would get out of the train, walk up, and there have Plymouth laid out before them – the wonderful vista up to the Hoe and the War Memorial. The city was virtually wiped out... there were five buildings left, and one of those didn't survive the planner – that was the Prudential Building. It was a huge...I can see it now...huge, red brick Victorian building, and that didn't survive. St Andrew's Church was gutted except for the towers that stood. The Western Morning News Office survived. The Odeon Cinema survived, the Prudential...and there was one other... but for practical purposes the city centre was wiped out. Royal Parade was meant to be much bigger than it is. You know on the Hoe side, they've got those flower beds? That was meant to be carriageway. They narrowed it from six lanes to four lanes, so they had spare lanes and put flowerbeds there. That's why Derry's roundabout is askew to Royal Parade!

Plymouth was to be the most beautiful city in Europe and become a benchmark for other cities.

Although I was a city councillor for forty-odd years, I wasn't involved as this was before my time. One interesting thing, which I often think of and makes me feel sad, is that Charles Church – the ruined monument – was going to be demolished so that the roundabout could be placed further up towards the Hoe. It was only kept by order of the council – I remember vividly that the idea was that the younger upcoming generation would not be able to conceive that a building could be blown up. That you wouldn't be able to *imagine* how a church could be damaged and look – people believed then that in the 'brave new world' it would *never* happen again. Of course, as we know sadly, that was a great disillusion.

I remember that the pre-fab houses were given a life of ten years, but they went on for forty or fifty years, and in the end there was much anger when the authorities had them demolished because people had made their own communities, in places like Whitleigh and Burrington, each with their own church and their own schools and pubs, and they were very happy like that. They were all down Tamar Way, on either side – from St Budeaux running to the Tamar Bridge.

I also remember that we weren't allowed to see films on Sundays – it was seen as the work of the Devil! The council had an angry debate after the war – a lot of anger was expressed – about cinemas being allowed to be open on Sunday.

Tom Savery

Image: Fotonow

Val Macleod, born in Plymouth, 1925. Lived in Mannamead and Cawsand during the war years:

Interviewer: Can you tell me some of your earliest memories?

I used to spend quite a lot of time with my paternal grandfather, who died when I was about four. He was my great friend and I called him 'Grandpa Beauty' for some reason – I don't know why! My father and I spent quite a lot of time with each other whenever he was back home from what was then the Army Political Service, because we both liked boats so we'd go off fishing together. I had my first very small rowing boat at the age of six, with lightweight oars, and my mother was horrified and thought I would probably drown to which Father would say, 'Don't be ridiculous. She can swim.' That was my main thing with him, we'd go off fishing and he'd take me on some extraordinary journey, once we spent two days away in a French crabbing boat and came back smelling to high heaven. I had a lot of fun with him.

Interviewer: Would you tell me about your job at the bank?

The bank was a very 'polite' place. No matter how bad the raids had been you couldn't go to work unless you were wearing a hat, and either wearing black, navy blue or grey. You had to have stockings on, and I would wear a pearl necklace, with pearl earrings, and colourless nail varnish – so we were very 'proper'. We were known as the 'young ladies of the Bank of England'. We used to get to work for ten o'clock in the morning and finish at four.

When I got up in the mornings to go to work, particularly after the Blitz, I'd have to walk from Mannamead to the bank – because you never knew if a bus was coming or not and if you did get on one, because of all the damage and rubble – how far would you get? It was a curious sort of life.

Interviewer: Where were you when you heard about the Declaration of War?

At Cawsand, in the sitting room, listening to the wireless. I sort of understood the gravitas but thought it was all very exciting; Father was with me – my mother wasn't there – and he was infuriated because they thought he was too old to be called up again. He was not happy about that.

Interviewer: Can you describe the house you were living in during the Blitz?

I was at Mannamead, it was a very big terraced house.

Interviewer: Can you give me your memories of the Blitz?

I spent a lot of time firefighting, and firefighting at night was a great thing because you never knew what was going to happen. I remember one particular night when my father and I were both working as fire-watchers. We'd arrived together and watched what was probably the first land-mine come down; it was a mine on a parachute. It came pretty close to us. I remember that my father, who was not a very emotional creature, looked at me, shook my hand, and said, 'Old girl, this is goodbye. I think this

one is for us.' Looking back, now, I don't think that statement particularly shocked me — I just thought, 'Oh well,
this is it!' It was a difficult time, the windows of our house
were blown out…and my mother was quite extraordinary
— she would *not* go into any shelter, or protect herself —
she'd just sit at her piano and play. She would play and
not even *notice* things were happening around her. We
went back to the house on one occasion and the whole of
the ceiling rose had come down, there was muck all over
the piano, and she was still playing away quite happily!
We never considered evacuation.

Interviewer: What did you think of the War itself?

I was never in any doubt that we would win. Obviously
there were times of great horror and misery. I remember
at the time of Dunkirk being down at Millbay Docks and
watching all these bedraggled soldiers and thinking, 'how
on earth are we ever going to get this together again?'

I remember helping out in a single-decker bus that had
been converted into a sort of canteen, and we'd go out
after the bombing and give tea to the people who were
clearing up or digging out, or whatever. I remember one
particular night we had taken the bus to Devonport, and
all of a sudden there was someone shrieking at us, 'Move
that vehicle! Move that vehicle!' We said, 'We can't!
We're serving tea! Why?' 'There's a bomb underneath
you!' they said. We moved…

Interviewer: What did you think of the Abercrombie plan
for the city centre?

I think, looking back, it was a brilliant job but sometimes too hurried. Royal Parade if you look at it is an absolute wind trap, but it's pretty splendid, and when you think it was the first city to be rebuilt...

Interviewer: Were you pleased with the speed of building?

Well materials were very hard to find. We were very lucky to have Lord Astor, who had a lot of power. He managed to find people and the materials to do the job.

***

I don't know if you have heard of the 'Boating Wrens'? Girls who were taken on to become sort of water taxis for the Services. They used to be in and out of the harbour all the time. If you can imagine Plymouth Sound absolutely crammed full with ships – everything had to be taken back and forth, mail, supplies, people – and frequently, bodies – had to be brought ashore. Those girls were quite extraordinary and had to brave an awful lot.

Val Macleod

Image: Fotonow

Vera Lavinia Evans, née Handcock, born 9th February 1934, in Weymouth:

My father had been an hotelier in London, and came down to Plymouth to be a publican. The Plymouth Breweries offered him two pubs – the Admiral McBride on the Barbican and the Elephant & Castle outside the Dockyard wall. Oh! Which pub do you think he chose? A bad mistake – he chose the one in Devonport, right by the Dockyard wall! So there we were, in 1939, and I can avidly remember that Sunday morning, 3rd September, I was eating a boiled egg in our kitchen, and war was declared. That's *so* vivid, that memory, and yet I was only five!

I have a poignant memory of the first night of the war. There was an iron gate at the bottom of the stairs to stop the customers wandering up them. We all went down to the bottom of the stairs – my father my mother, an aunt whose husband was away in Ceylon in the Army for five years, my sister who was about three, a tiny baby and me. We all had our gas masks on – and the baby was in the long 'cylinder' and one of us had the job of pumping air in to it; it was almost like an artificial lung. We actually heard the bombs on the first night of the war, there in Devonport. My mother, who always looked elegant and smart in the pub, was of the opinion *que sera sera,* so after going through that whole procedure on that first night she then said, 'Oh damn this!' and we never did it again throughout the rest of the war. Neither did she believe in us going to a shelter, one of the reasons being we were in a very, very busy Naval pub – my father had a perforated ear drum which I understand was from a bomb blast, and because of that he'd had to come out of the Navy – he always had a chip on his shoulder about that insofar as it prevented him from following the family Naval tradition. Then he went in the Military Police, but hated it because the very people he was searching for contraband were his customers! Once he was in full serge uniform, on a boat going up and down the River Thames and he fell in and he couldn't swim! The weight of his uniform was gradually dragging him down…he used to do boxing in the East End and that helped him control some our more rowdy customers, but otherwise I didn't really know much about my father.

The pub we lived in during the war was quite a big, tall establishment. On the ground floor was a big open bar, which was 'Men Only'. The counter was a long sweep of wood that was French polished every year. There was old-fashioned wainscoting on the walls, which was very practical, and the front door had the grain painted on every year. As the years went by the walls became absolutely yellow with smoke – everyone smoked in those days – there were hunting prints on the wall and a beautiful big mirror, which is now in my hall. The Bedford chair I have upstairs in the studio is one of those I saved from the 'Snug' which was 'Women Only'. Behind the counter was the trap door to the cellar and in those days the publican tapped his own barrels. Then you actually learnt the 'Art of Beer' as a trade. How it was made, tapped served, stored… It seemed that there was a lot more to being a publican than there is nowadays. There was another lounge-room downstairs… I used to hate the outside area, which had the gents toilets and always smelt awful, then the ladies toilets and the coal sheds – we had an awful lot of coal in those days. Also out there was a heavy wooden mangle, which I had to use when I was older to help Mother with the sheets. The middle floor had a large bedroom, and the kitchen, which was the hub of the house, had a large burner that burnt just about everything and kept it really, really warm. These rooms were cavernous and there was little heating – just a couple of gas fires. It was beautifully appointed with 1930s furniture that had come down from London. Upstairs I had a great, cavernous bedroom, and the walls always used to be damp. There were another two small rooms and a huge, very cold bathroom. But you couldn't have a bath because one of the directives, from the local authority, was that it should always be filled with water to put out any fires. So when we bathed, we had to use the tin ones and have a 'sink bath'. I remember putting Rex, my beautiful bob-tailed Old English sheep-dog, in there, getting him nice and clean only for matelots to steal him to sell to the American officers...who would take him to sea for months at a time! Then we'd spot him and have to pay to get him back again!

As you went along Park Street to the school, turned the corner and came along Aubyn Street, there was the Alhambra Theatre, which had many acts appearing. There was an Indian *fakir* who was a soothsayer and he would come into the pub selling silk scarves. One night he said to my mother that she would be surrounded by fire but that she would not leave – she would stay. In April 1941 on the night of the Blitz we were *completely* surrounded by fire. As I stepped out of the pub I saw there were incendiaries everywhere, there was *so* much fire. There was a Chief Petty Officer in the pub at that time... A couple of sailors picked up my sister and I – we had to get out of the pub because of the intensity of the fire and heat and my father being in the Dockyard and not around – and someone put helmets on our heads. My hair was burnt and we made our way to the water at Mutton Cove. When we got there I looked back and the whole of Devonport was ablaze. I remember my mother saying she never expected anything to be still standing because it was so severe, and there was burning rubble everywhere. She and my father had arrived back at the pub at almost the same time as each other, and discovered that it was still standing, and that it was the only building still standing in the street! Inside they found the Chief Petty Officer who had helped himself to a bottle of whiskey, rolled himself into a ball and slept right through the Blitz! The fakir was right – we did stay. There was no damage to the pub at all. Not even a pane of glass was broken! Incredible.

My mother never closed the pub down. It was open for the duration of the war, there was always someone around, they literally never shut it – if anyone wanted to stay there the night, then it was open for them. My aunt and mother ran that pub and worked extremely hard. My mother, so that we were in her sight during the raids, would put us in a bed down in the bar. During another raid two sailors picked me and my sister up but took us to different shelters. My mother was absolutely frantic – found my sister in one, and then they pulled me out of Devonport Market (which was near our school, in a huge cobbled square) and that very night it had a direct hit and three hundred people were killed down there. The pub was very central to the community, especially being a Naval pub. There was a woman down the road called Mrs Dellow, and she made the most amazing pasties loaded with meat – I've never tasted a pasty like it since! We managed well for food because when 'Aggie Weston's' (The Royal Sailors' Rest) was destroyed in the Blitz, the Dockyard built a huge American camp on the land and then we had a fantastic barter system going on; we had the beer, they had the big aluminum cans that used to hold salmon, fruit cocktail and ice cream! They were generous too, for example if it were my birthday the ship's cook would have a cake baked ready for me.

Devastated Devonport, with Aggie Weston's on the right.

So all the food would come across, and we'd invite all the children in the neighbourhood to the pub...there were many happy times and I was never, ever afraid.

We had farmer friends who lived at Tavistock, and apart from the food from the Americans, everyone bartered with their petrol coupons. We were middle-class, had a car, the business and voted Conservative. We'd swap clothing coupons for petrol coupons.

We remained in the Elephant & Castle pub until 1958, when the Dockyard put up a big wall and simply enclosed all that land.

*The Elephant & Castle pub, far right,
still standing after the bombing, Fore Street, Devonport.*

Vera Evans

Image: Fotonow

Victor French, born in Plymouth, 1939. Lived in Elm Road, Mannamead, Plymouth during the war:

My earliest memory is being carried into an air-raid shelter, which was in the garden of the one-bed flat we rented. We shared the bathroom with the landlord and his wife, who lived downstairs and that was fairly normal in those days. The Anderson shelter had two bunk-beds in it, and that's where we went to hide from the air-raids. I think at that age you have absolute reliance on your parents, and so events taking place around you are the norm. My father was in the RAF and my mother was at home, so I saw my father when he was on leave. I was an only child and my parents were very caring, it was as simple as that. I remember my grandfather very well. He was an ex-Navy man. He was a short, wiry chap and my grandmother was quite a large woman. One thing I particularly remember about them was that my grandfather brought home a parrot from South America, which was a bit of a highlight. We used to talk to the parrot, and the parrot would talk to us. Say things we'd never taught him – so I don't know what his background was!

I went to Margaret MacMillan's Nursery School, which is still there, on the Hoe. I can remember being taken out there for walks on the Hoe with the young ladies who looked after us. They were a big attraction, particularly for the American troops who were around in Plymouth. The Americans were very kind to us and gave us lots of sweets – probably to ingratiate themselves with the girls!

I can remember St Augustine's church being bombed,

because we went to Sunday School there, and there was a little farm at the end of the road, and that was bombed and all our windows were damaged – blown out, and there was a big Shire horse there that was killed in that particular raid, which we were all quite sad about.

After the war my parents tried desperately to get a council house as our accommodation was not particularly good, but they never had enough points…they probably didn't have enough children, actually, with just me, so we couldn't get a council house. I can remember Mother saying how envious she was of people who had got pre-fabs, as they were seen as the height of luxury then. It would have been nice to get one of those but we didn't. We subsequently moved, in 1949, to Salisbury Road, which was very much a nice, family neighbourhood, and you knew the local shopkeepers like the newsagents, the butchers, the guy who made pasties…and I belonged to the local Boys Brigade there. The St Jude's area has changed quite a lot since then, and most of the shops have gone. My father used to work in the Plymouth Gin Distillery, in Southside Street. He looked after the machinery down there, and he used to cycle to work from Salisbury Road.

I remember the friends I had there. We had access to the local parks and as kids we used to go there and play cricket – and football down at Tothill Park. I belonged to the local Boys Brigade in Salisbury Road, and I can remember a lot of the lads that were in that, and the camps we used to go to, and that kind of thing. I remember my great-aunt when she was looking after me, would occasionally take me to the 'Hyde Park' pub on Mutley Plain. Kids weren't allowed in, in those days, so I used to be concealed under the seat there, while my aunt drank a half of Guinness.

Down in Lipson, where the school is now, there was a big American camp. A lot of the youngsters used to go down there because the Americans were very kind and gave them all sorts of things. That was a bit of a highlight at the time. They were there for several years after the war.

I recall the victory celebrations in Elm Road. We used to have big things called 'static water tanks' in those days. I think it was if the mains water was interrupted in some way, by bombing, then the fire brigade could bail water out of these big tanks. There was one of these tanks just up the road from us and for the VE-Day celebrations somebody boarded it over. They got a load of planks and they just covered it over and that made a stage for the performances, and the local kids did various turns on the stage – singing or dancing. There was one girl up the road who quite an accomplished dancer and she danced on the stage. So, yes, we had quite a big street party. I can recall that as it was quite exciting. And I remember my mother saying that when the Queen visited Plymouth she actually spoke to me, so we must have been fairly near the front of the crowd. My mother always quite proudly told people, 'Yes, I pushed young Vic to the front, and the Queen spoke to him!'

After the war there was a temporary market that was set up nick-named 'Tin Pan Alley'. It was called that because all the stalls were formed of corrugated iron on scaffolding poles. When I was at school, at Public, there seemed to be plenty of building going on. There were two or three coffee bars that quickly sprang up in the '50s. There were a couple that were in old Nissen huts, temporary things, but yes, there seemed to be quite a bit going on and my father was actually able to get a mortgage to buy a house in Salisbury Road. It had what I think was called a 'restrictive tenancy', meaning there were two sets of tenants in the house that could not be moved, which meant to say that you could buy a house relatively cheaply – but that was the deal – you couldn't move them out, and you couldn't put up any rent. So the house was actually divided into three flats. We lived in one but we were the landlords – that was the difference, so yes, my life did change there, although we still took turns with the shared bathroom because there wasn't much that could be done about that, and money was still not that plentiful, but I was very happy in Salisbury Road. It was a good childhood there.

Vic French

Image: Fotonow

Vince Liddicoat, born 1929, Cattedown, Plymouth:

My earliest memory is from when my brother was born and I was about three years old. I remember my uncle was looking after me and we walked to the allotments that were down the end of the road. I was excited and shouted out to a farmer who was there, 'Hey mister! I got a baby brother home!' and I was so disappointed because he didn't take *any* notice of me, and I cried, 'He didn't listen to me!' to my uncle.

In my younger days we lived at 95, South Milton Street, Cattedown in what was called the Cheese House – there's a whole row of houses which looks similar to a block of cheese. My Grandmother was a Lucas. My father was a Liddicoat, it's a Cornish name but he was born here in Plymouth, in 1898 I believe, and worked for Esso's as a driver-salesman. We used to have a good family. We used to get a belt across the ear sometimes, I remember that - me and my brother! My father died in 1953 and he was only 55, I think. He had part of his lung cut away, in hospital in Bristol, as they did in those days, then he came home to where we were living in Laira. My mother's surname was Hughes, and she was the only one of her brothers and sisters that were born in Plymouth. She died when she was 90 years of age, of dementia.

We always had porridge, or cornflakes in the summertime, for breakfast. A roast on Sundays, cottage pie or cold meat on Monday – Mother would slice or grind up the leftover meat. I always had my desserts because I loved them! She used to do rice pudding, treacle pudding, tarts...she did all the cooking before the war. When the war came she took a job and used to drive a fifteen hundred-weight Army-type wagon and go out to the far end of Mutley Plain, then down to Peverell and out towards Crownhill, picking up food cooked for the communal canteens that the Government were running to help people in need out – the British Restaurants – so there would always be a canteen where you could get a subsidised meal. Her sister used to go with her. When war broke out Mother still managed to keep us well fed.

Mother learnt to drive when we all used to go out to Kingston, in my father's car – to the beach at Wonwell whenever there was a fine day – and she'd bake and wrap up pasties for those trips. There we used to meet up with my father's uncle, a couple of cousins, and friends as well – some lovely people – and we'd all mixed together and we'd come back and stop at Modbury, where the men went in to the pub for a pint and the women went and got chips for us, as they didn't drink.

I went to Cattedown School, but we were evacuated – we had relations in Roche, Cornwall, where my father originally came from, and my great-grandfather came from a place near Penzance, past Bodmin, near St Columb and he was called James Liddicoat. He married a girl from Roche. The two people looking after us – he was a coffin maker – had three sons and we were offered to go with a lady not far from St Dennis. The village where we went to school was called Whitemoor, we had to walk a mile to get there. The couple were called Brenton – the husband was called Harold Brenton – can't remember her Christian name. She was one of thirteen children. She was knocking on and they were two really lovely people. The first or second day we were going to school and we were joking around and laughing, and my brother said something funny and Harold chased him and poked him with a stick! Jokingly of course. It was a lovely place. I passed my exam and came home after a couple of years and then moved to Kingsteignton with my grandmother, and went to Torquay College for an engineering course.

There used to be a firm on the edge of Cattedown Quarry, a printing firm that used to print the *Herald* at one time. They had a big yard off South Milton Street and we had permission to use their air-raid shelter night times daytimes, whenever. We used to run down there, followed by Mother and Father carrying any necessities we might need, and we'd have been given a blanket or something to carry. I was ten years old and my sister was five years younger, and had to be helped along. I can't really remember the shelter, only that we could stretch out. The authorities visited us and told the adults what they could do to make their own shelters, such as tables with mesh around them and corrugated iron…but we went to the printing place's shelter.

We had a good life as children, Father was strict but he had very good points about him as well. He smoked and liked a pint, and he used to go to Salisbury Road Social Club just above the school – think it's still going – and meet my uncles and friends to play pool and darts. One day we saw this plane going over the houses and all these little dots coming down from it – that was the day they bombed the other end of South Milton Street. They were after the tanks at Esso, where my father worked as a driver salesman. We had a lucky escape. And a lot more bombs were dropped in our area so we evacuated.

My grandfather died in 1937 and I've got his barometer up there on the wall – it was presented to him for working in the Post Office. We used to go three times on a Sunday to Chapel in Tresillian Street, in Cattedown. I'm not saying we were religious but we just *had* to. Then afterwards we'd go in my Aunty Alma's for a bit of turnip – we liked that – a bit of raw turnip! Don't blame me if you try it and don't like it, mind you! I respected my parents and we were happy and had a good life. I had a lot of things that a lot of kiddies would have liked, and a good Christmas at home, every year.

There we are, it's been a lot of life! I'm glad we won the war, but of course many people lost their lives because one man was too greedy. As I've got older I just think I must enjoy myself as much as I can now.

William Lawrence Jean, born in Milehouse, Plymouth:

My mother was tall and slim, Father was of a stocky build and his hobby was doing water colours and black and white sketches; he was a very good artist. He drew a lot of places that were destroyed during the War, or since pulled down. Hundreds of drawings from around New Street and the Barbican harbour and various churches around the city. I have some tucked away somewhere.

I started school at the age of four, on Monday 28th August 1939. War was declared the following Sunday the 3rd September. I clearly remember Gran, who was visiting for the day, walking in and saying, 'War's been declared.' When my mother took me down to Hyde Park Primary School on the next Monday, all of us under-fives were sent back home until they'd built an air-raid shelter. I had just one week of schooling and didn't go back there until the following January, 1940! By then a shelter to accommodate all the school had been built in the rear playground. It had a flat top to it, there had been quite a big slope in the playground so you had to go up three lots of steps to get to the top and that then became the playground. From time to time teachers would stop the lesson and take us all down the shelter for 'shelter drill' so that if the worse came to the worse, and bombs dropped on one of the main entrances, we'd know how to make our escape up the ladders from one of the escape hatches. A five-year-old's legs aren't that long! You'd have to climb up a distance about the height of a room, and then assemble in the playground, where the teacher would count everybody off to make sure we were all accounted for, then we'd go back, and class would resume.

In 1941, on the first night of the Blitz, the school was very badly damaged. The whole of the top floor which accommodated the Seniors was burnt out completely, and the whole of the middle floor which accommodated the Juniors was burnt out. The two wings and the Infants on the ground floor, where I was, survived. I've still got vivid memories of when my mother took me down to school on that Friday morning after the night's Blitz and seeing the firemen's hoses going in – trying to save what was left of the school, and all the surplus water running down the slope, down the steps, down the tram-lines in Hyde Park Road and collecting at the bottom of Oxford Avenue.

There was a lot of water damage and the whole of the school was deemed unfit. I, and all the other infants, were schooled for two terms in the Sunday school rooms at Peverell Park Methodist Church, followed by two terms in the Hyde Park Social Club and then we were returned to our patched-up school in September 1942 when I went up into the Juniors and continued my schooling there. In those days it was three years in the Infants, and three years in the Juniors. As the hall – the middle part – had been burnt out, we couldn't walk from one end to the other as normal. We had to walk down all the steps, along the side of the shelter, and up steps the other end to get to the other wing of the Junior school. I remember taking the 11-plus in what proved to be the last year of the war, and our teacher Miss Millman saying, 'The war's coming to an end and this could be a real victory for you children if you pass your 11-plus!' Thankfully I did, and on Tuesday 11th September 1945 I went to Sutton High School in Regent Street, which is now converted into luxury flats, I understand. The school had been evacuated to St Austell during the war, but provision was made for those who hadn't wanted to go, or if the parents didn't want them to be evacuated, so they settled into what was known as the 'Emergency High School'. So boys from Devonport School and Sutton High, who hadn't been evacuated, were taught together. Mr Chesterfield, who was the Deputy Head at the time, became the Head Teacher of that Emergency High School. Regent Street was a very depressing road to walk along on the way to school – full of bomb-sites and pawnbrokers' shops and on a wet, drizzly morning everything looked grey and dismal.

My favourite food was a roast, and we always had Sunday roast. During the war years meat was rationed, I think at one point the ration came down to sevenpence a head for meat in the old currency so about 3p in new currency. Rabbits weren't rationed and they abounded, so you could get rabbit pie, which was nice in the winter months. In 1940 rationing came in and an aunt or uncle had been invited for tea one weekend, and I remember them saying, 'Well of course, food rationing comes in tomorrow,' and all the basics were rationed, like tea and sugar. Bread and cakes weren't rationed during the war until, I think, 1946 to '48, because the Canadians had a very bad wheat harvest and we imported from there. 1949 sweets were taken off the ration but there was such a rush for them that they had to be re-rationed! In 1950, we had a school trip to visit Windsor Castle and to go down the River Thames and I remember seeing a page from the *London Standard* saying petrol was being de-rationed, and that was five *years* after the war. All food rationing ended around May 1954.

There wasn't a lot of money in those days. My father worked very hard, and worked long hours, often collecting insurance premiums into the evenings, but there still wasn't much money coming in. He apparently had the worst book for insurance of that time because he had a lot of the old slum areas like Devonport, Stonehouse and the Barbican. I remember him telling me when I was growing up, of the appalling housing conditions and sights he'd seen. He was just collecting pennies and tuppences and premiums, and I don't know whether he got commission or a small wage but, like it was for most people, there was very little money around. We lived in a pleasant area of Peverell and it largely escaped the bombing.

Regarding house building after the war, there was a shortage of places for people to live and the Council were very strict with limits on the amount of private building that could be done. There was little private housing and it was many years before the Government relaxed the building restrictions. The Conservatives came back in in the 1950s and Harold Macmillan was the Housing Minister. He said that we would build 300,000 homes a year and apparently they did reach that target. In 1955 I went to work in the Housing Department of the City Council on the 'rents' side and there were *still* thousands on the council list waiting for housing, so there was a shortage even then. Ernesettle, Pennycross and Ham estates were all built from scratch in 1946 and '47. Whitleigh, at the time, was the biggest estate until Southway was completed. They kept spreading out. I can remember going to see one of the properties in Southway in 1957. I think it was in Frontfield Cresent – one of the first to be built – and seeing how tiny and pokey it was. It was generally known that houses weren't built to the standard that they had been before the war – for instance timber wasn't seasoned as it used to be. I can remember, as a child, seeing timber floating down in Stonehouse Lake, long before it became playing fields for Devonport School for Boys. The timber would probably be there for years getting seasoned, so it wouldn't shrink.

I think people were glad the city was being re-built as there had been so much congestion in the streets and it was nice with the trees on the parade but it lost its atmosphere and character. The rebuilding started exactly six years after the first night of the Blitz, apparently. We had some good members of Parliament, and they pushed it, from what I understand. Plymouth was ahead of re-building, going faster than any other city. Plymouth and Coventry were acknowledged as suffering the worse damage for their size. We were taken down from school on the 29th October, 1947 to see the King and Queen, who came to inaugurate the new building by unveiling the flagstaff on Royal Parade, which was later moved further up from where it originally was. Woolworths was the first store to open. Dingles had escalators and some people spent *all* day riding up and down them!

Interviewers
&
transcribers

This project has been supported by many kind people who gave up their time to help with organising, recording, transcribing and publicising, among other things.

We would like thank everyone involved, and if we have missed anyone out in error, please forgive us.

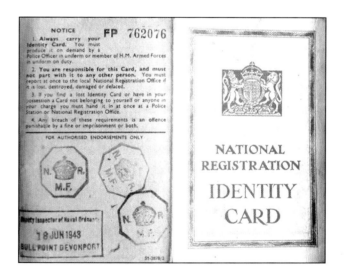

Interviewers:

Ailsa Griffiths

Adam Keelty

Alex Ashen

Clare Maudling

Catherine Reynolds

Danny Saxby

Dean Warren

Emily Cullen

Emma-Louise Collins

George Reed

Glyn Potter

Hope Grimson

Joshua Puleston

Kayleigh Luscombe

Paul Rimmer

Richard Ayres

Rosemary Babichev

Sam Rowe

Sue Baddeley

Tamsin Griffiths

Transcribers:

Carol Esom

Fiona O'Hanlon

Helen Pitcher

Joanne Geldart

Kerry Green

Nick Goodson

Sue Griffiths

Also thanks to:

Ian Pickard of www.deluxe7.com

John-Paul Somerville and the Lenkiewicz Foundation

Margaret Webb for her identity card

Ron Henwood for his *A Plan For Plymouth* Book

Vince Liddicoat for his copy of the bomb map

Vera Evans for her letter from the King

and everyone else who kindly allowed us to reproduce
some of their personal photographs

A final thank you once more, to Fotonow CIC
for their wonderful portraits

www.fotonow.org

NOTES

NOTES